First Moon

First Moon

MAUREEN THERESA SMITH

Celebration & Support for a Girl's Growing-Up Journey

New World Library
Novato, California

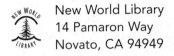

New World Library
14 Pamaron Way
Novato, CA 94949

Developed by Vanessa Brown
Copyedited by Laura Harger
Illustrations by Mari Gayatri Stein
Illustrations on pages 3 and 75 by Këri Bolding
Package design by Mary Ann Casler

Library of Congress Cataloging-in-Publication Data
Smith, Maureen.
  First moon : celebration & support for a girl's growing-up journey /
Maureen Smith.
      p.   cm.
  ISBN 1-57731-489-1 (pbk. : alk. paper)
  1. Menarche—Juvenile literature. 2. Puberty—Juvenile literature. 3.
Menstruation—Juvenile literature. I. Title.
  RJ145.S64 2005
  612.6'62—dc22   2004019822

First printing, January 2005
ISBN 1-57731-489-1
Printed in China

Distributed by Publishers Group West

10   9   8   7   6   5   4   3   2   1

CONTENTS

INTRODUCTION

When I was a little girl, I loved hanging out with my five older sisters. My perfect afternoon was spent sitting on their bedroom floor, a pile of their makeup spread out before me to play with, listening to them talk for hours about all the details of their lives: their friends, their boyfriends, their teachers, and their favorite music. I liked to be around them as they talked and played with one another, studied, prepared food, and got ready to go out on dates. It didn't really matter what they were doing; the fact was, they were teenage girls and I was totally fascinated with everything about them. I thought they were the coolest people ever. I liked to hear them talk about their bodies, about boys, and about their dreams. I loved the way they got ready to go out together, how they helped one another with their makeup and clothes, and I remember loving it when they let me braid their long hair. There was always music in the background, singing and dancing in front of the long mirror, and a lot of commotion as they prepared for a big night out. The ritual of getting ready was so fun that it felt like a celebration.

So much of my sisters' lives fascinated me. One of the most fascinating things was the care and comfort they offered one another during a few days of each month, and how they all seemed to feel pretty much the same way at the same time each month. I was curious about the mysterious boxes of pads and tampons I would find tucked away in the bathroom linen closet. I was also very aware that my mother expressed an understanding that I certainly did not have. When my sisters had cramps, she would give them medicine and speak to them in a quiet and concerned voice. Though I didn't understand these things, I was acutely aware of the unspoken connection that they shared. They all shared things that were still mysteries to me — a changing body and a "period," or as I like to call it, "moon" or "moontime." I was too young to menstruate, but I felt somehow connected, knowing that I too would one day have a period. And somewhere inside, I felt very proud of that.

The day I got my first moon wasn't such a big deal on the outside. The truth is, I had been so eager to be part of that mysterious womanly thing that I had lied to my friends and family, telling them I had started my period a year earlier. So, when I discovered a bit of blood on my uniform skirt on my way home from school at age thirteen, I was quietly elated. But I also felt a loss: I was unable to openly share this new experience in my life and to celebrate with my mom and sisters. I wished that I could go home and tell my sisters that I was now officially "one of them." I soon realized, however, that none of my friends were celebrating the arrival of their periods either.

Years later, in college, I studied women's history and women in many cultures. I learned some really cool things. Did you know that since the beginning of civilization, many cultures around the world have celebrated a young woman's first moon with dancing, gifts, and festivities?

For a Native American girl from California coastal tribes, menarche (another word for the first moon or period) was an occasion for intense attention from her family and her village. In the fall, a special dance to honor several girls' menarches brought groups of neighboring villagers, who arrived with gifts, food, and singing. The festivities lasted five days. In Brazil, a young woman's first period is celebrated with a parade of flowers. When I learned this, I thought, that's the way to enter your womanhood!

I have come to believe that celebrating your changing body and celebrating yourself are key to happiness, fun, and creativity in life. Celebrating with friends and family and sharing stories and traditions are part of what makes being a girl and becoming a woman so rich, full, and magical.

So, this book is all about celebrating this incredible time in your life — a time when you are growing from the beautiful girl you are now into the amazing woman you were born to be. It is also about making sure you have the tools you need to create a life full of happiness, wisdom, magic, and celebration for yourself. I hope that this book helps to ensure that you have everything you need to discover yourself and to become all you dream of being. Women are magical. You are the magic. Celebrate yourself on the special day when you have your first moon. You are a magical, magnificent woman!

chapter 1

THE MENSTRUAL CYCLE
Preparing for Moontime

The first moon is an experience that all women go through, though your personal journey is unique to you. The nice thing is that because all women have or have had periods each month, we are all united in the experience of the menstrual cycle. On the occasion of your first moon, you become part of the ever-growing and ever-changing circle of women.

I honor and celebrate you today with the following stories, exercises, and wisdom, all meant to support, nurture, inspire, and accompany you as you grow during this first year of your cycle. Most important, remember that you are celebrated each and every day. Because of you, the world is a better place.

Moontime Mythology

Many girls learn about and celebrate their first moon by hearing stories about menstruation from other girls and women. Sometimes it's fun to create your own moontime myths. Here is a moontime myth created by a mom to explain menstruation to her two daughters.

"THE GODDESS MENSES," BY MARGE ROSENTHAL

Once a month, the Goddess Menses visits a woman's body. She is a very mysterious goddess. Sometimes she sneaks in without us knowing, and sometimes she announces herself with powerful tuggings inside our bodies. When men bleed, it is always a sign of illness or injury, but the bleeding the Goddess Menses brings is a reaffirmation of life, a cleansing of our bodies. Her arrival is a time of celebration, a time to buy flowers or something small and special just for us women. The Goddess Menses is a high-spirited, energetic goddess who plays tricks on our bodies, arriving early or late, quiet or stormy, and tugging or rolling over us, but once her presence is acknowledged, she is very happy to settle down and wait...until next time.

What Happens When You Menstruate

UNDERSTANDING THE BASICS

To best understand what is happening when you menstruate, it is important to first have a general understanding of your body. All girls and women have special organs inside and outside our bodies that developed before we were born, as we were growing inside our mothers' wombs. Now that you are growing from a girl into a young woman, these organs are beginning to develop and mature, too. These organs are generally referred to as the organs of the female reproductive system, or *genitalia*. To best learn about these special organs, you can look at the following illustration as you read along or, if you like, use a small hand mirror to look at your own genitalia.

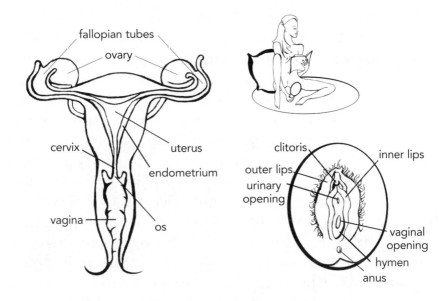

fallopian tubes

ovary

cervix

uterus

endometrium

vagina

os

clitoris

outer lips

urinary opening

inner lips

vaginal opening

hymen

anus

The organs on the outside — the parts of your body you can see just by looking between your legs — are the *external female genitalia*. A more common name for the external female genitalia is the *vulva*. The outermost part of the vulva is the outer lips, or *labia majora*. During puberty, the time when your body is changing from a girl's into a woman's, pubic hair will start to cover these outer lips. Inside or sometimes protruding from the outer lips are the inner lips, which are also called the *labia minora*. These lips might be pink or brown; they might have some blue or purple areas; and they might be larger, the same size as, or smaller than the outer lips. The inner lips might be wrinkled or smooth. All these variations are normal. Every girl is unique, and there are as many differences in the lips' size, shape, and color as there are girls in the world. Toward the top of the inner lips is the *clitoral hood*. Just beneath it is the *clitoris*. It is a very small organ. The clitoris is filled with thousands of nerve endings that make it very sensitive and can create good physical feelings and arousal — meaning sexual feelings. It will continue to grow and become more sensitive as you develop.

Below the clitoris is a very small opening called the *urethra*. This is where your urine passes from your bladder. Just below the urethra is the *vaginal opening*. This is the opening to the internal reproductive system and organs. In many girls, the opening is partially covered by the *hymen*, which is a thin tissue. Many other girls are born without this tissue, and the hymens of some girls have been stretched or torn from exercise. Whether you have a hymen or not, you are normal. The vaginal passageway is very important. It is a moist entryway that leads to the internal genitalia. First, it leads to the *cervix*. The cervix is small, with a little indent, called the *os*, in its center. The os is the opening to another small organ, the *uterus*. When a woman gives birth, this tiny opening grows large enough for a baby to pass through, but the rest of the time it stays very, very small. The uterus is hollow and has a lining of tissue called the *endometrium*. The uterus is special because it stays small except when a woman is pregnant, but then expands to hold the baby during pregnancy. Once the baby is born, the uterus shrinks back to its regular size.

Extending from the top of the uterus are two tubelike projections, the *fallopian tubes*, which connect to two small organs called *ovaries*. The ovaries produce a hormone, *estrogen*, that is responsible for your body changing from a young girl into a young woman. The ovaries also contain eggs, or *ova*. The ova contain each woman's genetic information, which will become part of the genetic makeup of a new baby. Girls have approximately 250,000 eggs in their ovaries, and these begin to mature during puberty. A mature egg is released each month from an ovary and travels through one of the fallopian tubes to the uterus. This is called *ovulation*. If the egg is met by a male sperm cell, released from a male's penis, this combination of egg and sperm — called the *fertilized* egg — will then attach itself to the walls of the uterus, where it is nourished by the endometrium, the blood-rich tissue inside the uterus mentioned earlier. This is called *pregnancy*. If the egg isn't fertilized — which means there is no pregnancy — it disintegrates. The endometrial tissue, which has been building up to nourish a fertilized egg in pregnancy, also disintegrates. The tissue passes out of the body as the menstrual flow each month.

WORDS AND DESCRIPTIONS FOR MENSTRUATION

Many terms are used to discuss menstruation: *menstruation, menses, menarche, period, menstrual cycle,* and my favorites, *first moon* and *moontime.* I will go through each of these terms with you so that you'll understand what people are referring to when they use the terms and to help you understand more about your body. There is also a complete glossary of terms in the back of this book.

- **menarche, or first moon:** *Menarche,* or *first moon,* are terms that describe the first time a young woman experiences menstruation. Menarche, or first moon, usually happens between the ages of nine and fourteen, although it can occur earlier or later. The time menarche arrives has a lot to do with your heritage — asking your mother, grandmothers, aunts, and sisters when they began their periods can give you an idea of when your first moon might occur.

- **period, menses, moontime, and menstrual flow:** *Period, menses,* and *moontime* refer to the three to seven days a month when your body releases menstrual fluid. *Menstrual flow* is another term for menstrual fluid.

- **menstruation and menstrual cycle:** The terms *menstruation* and *menstrual cycle* refer to the total monthlong process described above. Your period is the first phase of your cycle. During the second phase, your body produces more estrogen, which makes endometrial tissue grow. The third phase, *ovulation*, is when an egg is released from an ovary. In the fourth phase, your body produces another hormone, called *progesterone*, and more estrogen, which continue to grow the endometrium. If the egg isn't fertilized, the body makes less of these hormones and the endometrial lining sheds along with a small amount of blood — and the menstrual flow or period begins again. The whole menstrual cycle usually takes approximately twenty-eight days; however, it is normal to have shorter or longer cycles. When you are just beginning to menstruate, it might be that you experience only a few periods in your first year instead of one each month, as it can take some time for your body to develop and adjust to new changes. You can keep track of your cycles using the Flow Chart and stickers in this kit.

Menstruation is a healthy and normal part of life. Menstruation happens for a very important reason: it is part of the reproductive system. Every month, your body begins to prepare itself for a possible pregnancy. Even though pregnancy is not something young girls are ready to prepare for, menstruation is how the body develops and gets ready for a possible pregnancy someday. Following the natural cycle and rhythm of menstruation can support you as you prepare for all kinds of other newness in your life: new interests, new dreams, and new visions. I will talk more about this in later chapters.

The Moontime Starter Kit:
Supplies You Will Need When You Start Your Period

Preparing for your first moon is an easy and fun thing to do. If you have already had your first moon, then preparing for your next moontime can help make your period fun, effortless, and comfortable.

Since it's hard to know when your menstrual flow will begin, the best thing to do is to create a moontime starter kit. The important thing to remember is that if you are not prepared, don't worry. All women have had their period. It's a natural, healthy part of life, and you will be able to get the help, advice, and supplies you need no matter where you are.

A MOONTIME STARTER KIT STORY

My friend Tory had an amazing nanny named Maria. She was from Germany and spoke little English. She took care of Tory and her siblings while their parents worked. Maria always made sure Tory and her sisters and brothers had everything they needed as they left the house for school each day. One of the sweetest gifts Maria gave Tory was a small, beautifully decorated zippered cloth case. Tory carried it in the outside pocket of her backpack. I was always curious about what was inside, but Tory was private about her bag from Maria.

One day in the girls' bathroom, she asked me to get it out of her backpack for her. She let me see what was inside. The case carried a few menstrual pads (two thick pads and one thin), an extra pair of underwear, a small medicine box with a few pain-relief tablets, and a little note on red stationery from Maria to Tory that read, "Take special care of yourself today. Be gentle and listen to your body. Pay attention to your dreams. This is your special woman time."

I thought this was one of sweetest gifts I had ever seen. I was also very interested in the message about paying attention to your dreams that Maria had included. I had no idea why she would say this or how it was connected to having a period, but it struck me as important somehow. It was more of the moontime mystery that I had found so intriguing with my sisters. I decided I wanted to make a moontime kit for myself, and I pretended that it was from a wise and mysterious aunt, who, in my imagination, would continue teaching me the mysteries of being a woman.

You and your mom, sisters, or friends can customize a moontime supplies case and include whatever you desire in it. You can find carrying cases at most drugstores, usually in the toiletries section — or you can make your own.

SUGGESTED ITEMS TO INCLUDE IN A MOONTIME STARTER KIT

1. A reminder just for you: this could be a nice note to yourself, a special stone, or jewelry that reminds you to take special care of yourself today.

2. Two or three pads (thick and thin, depending on how heavy or light your flow is).

3. An extra pair of underwear (in case you leak).

4. A few pain-relief tablets (with your doctor's permission).

5. Essential oils with soothing scents, to massage onto cramped areas.

6. Warm strips for cramps (see page 14).

7. If you're expecting your very first moon, include a "get out of school free" card just for this first day. This gives you permission to call your mom, dad, or guardian to

pick you up if you need to be home or to do something special for yourself today.

If you are uneasy about the possibility of getting your period at school, you could also pack a sweatshirt or an extra pair of jeans or shorts in your backpack. You will probably feel the menstrual fluid long before it reaches your outer clothes, but if it does soak through, it usually will be a very small amount that can be easily covered by tying a sweatshirt around your waist. When I had my first period, I was walking to the bus stop, wearing my school uniform skirt. A little fluid did leak onto my skirt, but I was able to wrap my sweatshirt around my waist until I got home.

Tampons, Pads, and More: How to Pick What's Best for You

For thousands of years, women have used all kinds of things to catch their menstrual flow — from tree moss to leaves to cloth rags to modern pads and tampons. Many choices are available to girls and women today. They are advertised as *feminine hygiene products* or *menstrual protection products*. With so many choices, you are free to experiment and select the products that work best for you.

Living in a house full of big sisters, I was aware that there were all kinds of products for girls to choose among when they got their periods. Sometimes I would spend time alone or with my best friend sitting on the bathroom floor, secretly reading all the instructions and looking at the diagrams and illustrations that came with the pads or tampons. I wanted to figure it all out — periods, my body, how it would work — and I also wanted be sure that I knew what the best products were. I also wanted to use what seemed "coolest" or most advanced or trendy. What I discovered, when I finally did get my period, was that there is no one "cool" product. I liked to use both tampons and pads, in different sizes and styles, at different times during my period. Some of my preferences have changed over time as my own life, body, and needs have changed. When it comes to being cool, cool means what works best for you. If you feel comfortable, secure, and good, then you are happy. And that's cool.

Another way to figure out which products are best for you is to choose a certain type or brand of tampon or pad. This might be the first time you make a decision about how you wish to spend your money as a consumer of products made just for women. You will now have many opportunities to consider which women's items you want to buy. Your awareness and personal values might grow as you think about what is important to you when you spend your money. For example, when I was a young woman, I did not know about products that were better for the environment and my body than others, products labeled "environmentally safe" or "bio-degradable" or "organic." But, just as I have learned over time about the importance of taking good care of my body, I have also learned about an important responsibility: to care for Earth's body. Now I am aware that I can purchase organic tampons. It is important to me to use products that are not harmful to the environment or my body. Products free of chemicals and products that biodegrade disintegrate over time and do not create waste. Whenever possible, I choose to buy organic, environmentally safe products. When choosing the right menstrual products for yourself, these issues might also be important for you to consider.

There are several types of products on the market, and new ones appear all the time. Following are general descriptions and tips on those products I know best; however, you might find other types that are not listed here. Feel free to peruse the shelves in the feminine hygiene section, take your time reading labels, and never be embarrassed to purchase the supplies you need. I recommend a shopping spree, or a swapping spree with friends. You might want to try out each type of product to discover for yourself which products you like best. You can also ask your mom and your friends which products they like best and why. I have provided a list of resources that includes helpful books, websites, and information on feminine hygiene products at the back of this book.

ALL ABOUT PADS

Pads offer a soft, thick layer of material for absorbency. They come in different sizes, and some even have adhesive "wings" designed to protect your panties. Here are some descriptions of the different types of pads to choose from:

- Minipads (small and used for light flow) and maxipads (thick and used for heavy flow) are easy to use. Both kinds have adhesive tape on the bottom side of the pad that sticks onto your underwear during your period. Maxipads are best for a heavy flow and can provide extra protection overnight. Some girls need to change their pads several times a day, others just a couple of times, depending on their flow.

- Pads with wings are made to further protect your panties and prevent staining. Generally, however, I find that when I have my period, I do get some blood on my underwear during the first couple of days.

- Reusable cotton pads are an option, especially if you are seeking comfort and environmental consciousness. As Lynda Madaras points out in *The What's Happening to My*

Body Book for Girls, women in the United States use approximately 12 billion menstrual pads each year. If you were to lay them end to end, the pads would stretch 1.6 million miles. That's enough for three round-trips to the moon! Seven billion tampons go into landfills, sewers, and waterways every year. Cotton pads are both comfortable and nonpolluting. You can soak a used pad in water and then launder it in the washing machine. Many companies sell airtight carrying cases for used pads. Like other pads, these come in different shapes, sizes, and styles. You can find them at most health food stores or online.

- Panty liners are very thin pads and not as useful as thicker pads during your period, but they can come in handy on light-flow days as your period tapers off. Some women like to use them to protect their panties during other times of the month if they experience a lot of *vaginal discharge* (a clear or whitish fluid that is released between periods, especially during ovulation).

ALL ABOUT TAMPONS

Tampons are another option for absorbing menstrual blood. A tampon is different from a pad in that it is used inside the vagina. It is a small cotton tube or plug with a string hanging from one end. Some brands have a plastic or cardboard applicator for inserting the tampon, and some are designed to be inserted with your finger. A tampon is inserted into the vagina to absorb the blood before it leaves the vagina. Once it has absorbed all that it can hold (usually after four hours), you take the tampon out by pulling the string.

Tampons cannot get lost or go "too far" into the vagina. As

mentioned above in the description of the reproductive system, the cervix is very small, too small for a tampon to fit through. After a tampon is used, it should be wrapped in toilet paper and thrown away (not flushed).

Depending on the lightness or heaviness of your flow, you might need different sizes of tampons (thick for heavy flow, thin for light flow), as with pads. Tampons are especially useful if you plan to swim or engage in athletic activities, when you don't want menstrual blood to leak. Many companies sell organic tampons and tampons with biodegradable applicators.

If you aren't sure about the right time to begin using tampons, it is a good idea to check with your mom and/or your doctor. Here are some other important things to know about the safe and effective use of tampons.

Every tampon box contains a warning about *toxic shock syndrome* (TSS). TSS is a rare illness that occurs when bacterial toxins from the vagina enter a girl's or a woman's bloodstream, causing her to become very sick or, in some extremely rare cases, causing death. Symptoms of TSS include fever, vomiting, diarrhea, lightheadedness, aching muscles, headaches, and a rash that looks like a sunburn. It is an illness that progresses quickly, but it can be treated effectively if caught early. TSS can develop when tampons are used, especially if they are not used correctly. If you or anyone you know experiences these symptoms while using a tampon, it is important to remove the tampon and call a doctor.

The best method for preventing TSS is to use the smallest size of tampon necessary to absorb your flow. This could mean using different sizes over the course of your period. Another important practice is to change your tampon frequently, waiting no longer than every two to four hours. A healthy approach to preventing TSS is to use pads as often as possible, particularly at night.

OTHER PRODUCTS TO CONSIDER

- **Warmstrips or heatwraps** are air-activated adhesive pads that you can place on your lower abdomen to comfort and soothe cramping. You can find them at the grocery store along with other menstrual supplies.

- **Essential oils** (which I discuss further in chapter 5) can also be extremely soothing during moontime. Some of my favorites to soothe cramps are roman chamomile and lavender. You can place a few drops in the palm of your hand and gently massage them onto your lower abdomen. Or just use them to soak in a bubbly tub. Essential oils can be found at your local health food store.

PERSONAL PREFERENCES

After I had my first moon, I used pads for the first few months. This gave me a chance to learn about my menstrual flow and its rhythm. By the time summer came around, I wanted to be able to swim, and I was ready to try tampons. I started with a "slender" or "junior" size that is made specifically to be comfortable for a young woman trying tampons for the first time. I asked two of my girlfriends to demonstrate how to use a tampon. Once they had shown me, we showed another friend. It seemed tricky at first. Instructions are included with a tampon box, but it was really helpful — and pretty funny — to learn from my friends. It was a bonding experience that illustrated the importance of female friendships.

Good Ways to Take Good Care: Friends, Stories, and Advice

"GOING GREEN," BY FIONA, AGE SIXTEEN

When I learned about organic tampons and reusable cotton pads, I started using them because I wanted to do my part to protect the environment. Cotton pads are very soft and comfortable. I like the way they feel more than regular pads, and I like the benefit to the environment. I didn't like having to soak and wash them at first — it seemed inconvenient and kind of gross — but after a while, I started liking them because I feel so much better about being a woman and taking care of my body and the Earth.

"NAPS AND COMFORT," BY MARY, AGE FOURTEEN

When I first started getting my periods, I took lots of naps because I thought that way, when I woke up, I'd have less time to spend actually, consciously *having* it. I got my period really young, and I wasn't quite ready for the whole growing-up thing yet.

Oh, and *elastic waistband pants*. I don't even bother with jeans during that time of the month. I just let myself stretch out.

"WHY I LOVE TAMPONS," BY WENDE, AGE THIRTY-SIX

When I first got my period, in sixth grade, my mom gave me a pad. Then my friend invited me to go swimming, so I asked my mom how I would do that, and she said, "You don't." So I went with a pad but couldn't go in the pool. The other girls kept asking me why I wouldn't go in, and when I finally told them, one said, "Why don't you use a tampon?" I didn't even know what they were, and it would take me another three years to figure them out!

Finally, in ninth grade, I met this girl that I really liked. One of the first ways we bonded was by learning that we were both afraid to put tampons in — so we decided to help each other figure it out. That summer, we happily hit the beach with our newfound freedom and learned to surf!

Moon Wear

Most of my friends have a pile of raggedy undies stashed away in their underwear drawers that they save to use during their periods. But I suggest treating yourself to seven pairs of ultra-comfortable cotton panties just for your moontime. That way, you have super-comfy, stain-acceptable panties for your moontime, and you can save your other, favorite undies for the rest of the month.

MOONTIME MOMENTS: DECORATE YOUR OWN MOON WEAR

Start a fashion trend among your girlfriends by designing your own moon wear. Here's how:

1. Start with a little shopping. First, purchase five to seven pairs of comfy 100 percent cotton (or even better, 100 percent organic cotton) underwear.

2. Next, purchase some fabric paint and paint fixative. Both are readily available at your local crafts store and come with directions for use. They are super-affordable and easy to use. You might also find some cool iron-ons.

3. When you get home, wash and dry your new panties.

4. Set up a space in your home where you can be creative. Lay some newspaper down to protect the surface you are working on. Be sure it is fully covered so that it's safe from paint stains.

5. Add a bit of fixative to your paint, according to the label directions, to prevent the paint from running later in the washing machine.

6. Go for it! Design the moon wear of your dreams. Paint the phases of the moon or a sprinkling of stars; write the word MOON or the days of the week across the back of your undies. (Did you know that Monday means "Moon-day"?)

7. Let dry for seven days.

8. Wash inside-out and line-dry. (It is always best to line-dry clothing that has been treated with fabric paint.) Enjoy!

chapter 2

CELEBRATION
Honoring Your First Moon

I celebrate your passage into young womanhood. Because of you, the world is blessed. The Navajo believe that at the time of menarche a young woman brings gifts to her people and that everything she touches is blessed with her womanhood. Your first moon is a magical time. Celebrating your first moon in a way that is special to you is a way to love and honor the amazing girl you are.

Celebrating Transitions

Changes and transitions, times when you are growing from one phase of your life into the next, are parts of life that we can always count on. Sometimes they are easy, and other times they are not so easy. All kinds of feelings can be attached to transitions. Sometimes you might feel really excited about growing up. Other times you might hate it and want to stay a kid forever. You might like your changing body but also feel awkward and not quite comfortable in it yet. You might like the idea that your body is beginning to change into a beautiful womanly shape, but you might also miss your wonderful child shape. Your first moon signifies this time of change in your life. It's a time to celebrate your kid self, your between-kid-and-woman self, your entering-into-womanhood self — and all the feelings and dreams that come with them.

Celebrating your first moon might be one of many celebrations of passages in your life, and it might be the first of many "in-between" stages, too. For thousands of years, in cultures all over the world, a young woman's first moon has been seen as such an important time in her life that special celebrations and festivities mark this moment of growth, beauty, and change. Celebrate yourself today! You are a beautiful and amazing girl.

Moontime Mythology: A Navajo Celebration

The Navajo people celebrate the connection between a girl's first moon and succeeding passages in her life, like childbirth and old age. During her puberty ceremony, the girl is dressed in the image of Changing Woman, the most powerful Navajo deity. She wears beautiful, colorful clothing and is decorated with turquoise jewels. Turquoise is Changing Woman's sacred stone and is associated with the Earth. As the girl is dressing, a song of reverence and celebration is sung to her by the women in her tribe. The song tells her of the treasured jewel she is for herself and her people. The association with Changing Woman reminds the girl that her life is always changing and in transition, and that there are many phases of life.

Girls and Moms Share Their Moontime Experiences

Celebrating your first moon in a way that is just right for you is important. There are many, many possibilities. Some girls like to go out to lunch and spend an afternoon shopping with their mom or "other mom" (an "other mom" is any trusted adult woman in your life whom you can share things with); others might like to invite a circle of women and girlfriends over for a first moon ritual celebration. Still others might see their first moon celebration as tying in well with another coming-of-age ceremony or ritual, such as a bat mitzvah or confirmation.

KERI'S STORY

Keri decided she wanted to celebrate by having a slumber party with four of her girlfriends, her mom, and her aunt. They made a special "moontime meal" together. The table was beautifully set with candles, flowers, Keri's favorite foods, and wish boxes. The girls each took turns writing their wishes for Keri and placing them in her wish box. Then they wrote wishes for themselves and filled their own. For dessert, they created a "wish cake" borrowed from another family tradition. Hidden in the cake were three silver dollars representing the wealth and gifts of Keri's dreams. After dinner, the girls and women each told stories about their first moons and how girls can care for themselves during their moontime. They painted their nails, ate good food, and giggled late into the night.

Moontime Meditation

In India, when Nayar girls have their first moons, they sit in seclusion to meditate on their new womanly status before they are dressed in a new sari by their female neighbors, taken to a ceremonial bath, and given a feast. You might like to try meditation for yourself at this special time.

WHAT IS MEDITATION?

Some people say that meditation is the best way to become best friends with yourself! Meditation is a way to give yourself a time-out from the world, tune in to your own thoughts and feelings, calm down, and feel good. It's a simple way to relieve stress and tension, be comfortable in your body, balance your emotions, and easily revive your energy and creativity. It's also a way to get quiet and just be. Meditating at the time of your moon — and during other times of change — is an easy and fun way to take good care of yourself. It is a practice that people in many cultures have used for centuries to help themselves relax and find internal calm, no matter what is going on in the external world. It is a way to bring good things into your life by taking time to imagine how you would like your life to be and how you want to feel.

MINI-MOONTIME MEDITATION: A FIRST MOON CELEBRATION

The following is what's called a *guided meditation* or *guided imagery. Guided* means that you read or listen to a story while you're really relaxed and let your imagination follow along. Its only difference from reading a regular story is that you can use it to gain more insight into your own thoughts and feelings.

Before you begin, you might want to ask your mom, dad, another family member, or a woman friend to read this to you as you relax with your eyes closed. Or you could make an audio recording of yourself reading it very slowly before you begin. If you can't do either of these things, read through the meditation first, then lie down and imagine it in your mind, taking your time.

When you are ready, find a comfortable place to relax, lying down flat or sitting up with your eyes closed. Take a few deep breaths. Feel your chest rise and fall with your breath. Imagine all your thoughts and worries from the day leaving your body with each exhalation. As you breathe in, imagine that your body is filled with warmth, love, and calm.

Imagine yourself walking down a beautiful forest path. It is an enchanting moonlit night. You have no trouble seeing because the full moon is so bright that it lights the path for you to follow. Your closest friends surround you. In the near distance you hear other girls and women singing. As you walk toward this sound, you are filled with anticipation and excitement. The singing gets closer and closer. Just in front of you, you see a clearing lit by the full moon.

As you walk into the clearing, two girls, who are just a year or so older than you, greet you and your friends. They hand you beautiful flowers and place a crown of flowers on your head. Taking your hands, they guide you into the center of a circle made up of many girls and women. As you look around, you see the faces of women from every part of the world, of all ages, singing you a beautiful song of celebration and welcome. You realize that even though each woman sings in her native language, together their voices are in perfect harmony and the words make perfect sense to you. The music is so beautiful and you are so happy that you and the other girls and women start to dance. Looking around at all the women in the circle with you, you begin to see your connection to them and your connection to the Earth, the moon, and the stars. As the singing ends, your eyes fall on one of the women.

Her gaze meets yours, and she smiles. She has a special gift for you. Her gift is from all the women in the circle. It contains the wisdom shared by all women for all ages. She comes to you and offers you the special gift. Take time now to receive your gift. Imagine that it is words, a symbol, or a song — and whatever it is, it is just for you. Take your gift to your heart. Place your hands over your heart. This is your welcome into the greater circle of women. This circle is always here for you. It is your own special place to come and receive wisdom and understanding any time you might need it in your life. This circle lives in your heart. Allow yourself time to rest here, listening to anything else the woman or women have to say.

When you are ready, imagine looking up to the sky to see the moonlight disappearing and the dawn of the new day arriving. This new day begins a new phase of your life. You are filled with happiness, love, and strength. You know that you are never alone and that you have generations of women to love, support, and assist you as you grow.

And now begin to bring your awareness back to today, carrying with you your gift and memories from this special celebration. Remember that you can return to this circle of women's wisdom whenever you need to, just by asking and touching your heart.

And when you feel ready, wiggle your toes, take a deep breath, and open your eyes.

Moontime Journaling

This book has a companion journal that you can use as your own personal moontime journal. You can write about anything you like in it. Some girls like to use their journals to record their daily thoughts and the events of the day. Some girls think of their journals as good friends who listen to all their thoughts, feelings, dreams, and fears, and they can talk to their journals without any fear of judgment or worry that someone else might hear their words.

Moontime journaling can be especially fun because during your moontime, you might often find that your dreams are more vivid or easier to remember, or because you might feel especially reflective or creative and want a place to write. It might also be a place where you can start to record all kinds of other stuff: your moontime meditation experiences, your own moontime stories and myths, details about the way your body feels during your cycle or what kinds of food you eat — things that you notice help you feel good during your moontime.

MOONTIME MOMENTS: JOURNAL REFLECTIONS

1. Take out your moontime journal. Write about your first moon celebration meditation (see above). What was it like? How did you feel? What friends and women did you recognize in your meditation? Did you like the experience? Is meditation something you would like to try again?

2. List ten things that you like about yourself. Then acknowledge and celebrate these special qualities by hanging a copy of the list on your mirror.

Planning Your First Moon Celebration

How would you like to celebrate your first moon? Would you like a special dinner? A ceremony with friends and family? To shop for something special that's just for you? Take out your journal and write about what you would like. Then share your celebration wish with your mom, other mom, or girlfriends. It's nice to have at least one older woman around, someone who has already had the experience of her period, so that she can help you to celebrate as well as answer any questions you might have.

The best thing about this celebration is that it is all for you, and you get to ask for exactly what you want. You might want to have a dinner party with a few special girls and women, such as your friends or your aunts, sisters, mom, and grandmothers. Or you might like the idea of an adventurous full-moon hike with your dad, mom, and friends.

Another great way to celebrate is to have a first moon celebration ritual. First moon rituals or coming-of-age ceremonies are created to acknowledge and celebrate this important time of growing from a girl to a woman. Rituals may include objects like candles, flowers, and stones that hold symbolic meaning to you and your family: a candle representing warmth and light, flowers mirroring your beauty and growth, a stone symbolizing the Earth.

Rituals give family members and friends an opportunity to show their love for you and remind you of the great circle of support that surrounds you as you grow.

What do you want your ritual to be like? As you think about what to include, ask your family and friends for their ideas. Maybe you want to dress up in a brilliant red dress and adorn yourself with flowers and jewelry. Maybe you want to stand in the center of a circle and receive good wishes from your family and friends. You could bring some items into the circle with you that represent different phases of your life, such as a rattle from when you were an infant, your stuffed animal from toddler years, a trophy from your first soccer tournament, or some photographs. You could also bring a description of the woman you are seeking to become. It is a powerful experience to acknowledge the different phases of your life while surrounded by the people who love you, and to voice your dreams to these witnesses. In doing so, your dreams are born and held in the sacred circle of your friends and family, and as their love nurtures you, your dreams are able to come to life.

There are many ways to create rituals. In the resources section at the back of this book, I have included contact information for purchasing First Moon Ceremonial Kits, created by Helenya Brooke. The kits include instructions and items that help you to create a beautiful first moon ritual.

Moontime Munchies

Moontime is a time to eat healthy foods and really nourish your body. It is also a time when some girls experience cravings for salty foods or chocolate. In chapter 3, I'll talk about nutrition and moontime body care. But for your moontime celebration, it might be fun to try a special "goody" recipe. Maybe your celebration could include baking with your mom and your friends. Here is a delicious and fun recipe for one of my favorite treats.

Many Moons Cupcakes

INGREDIENTS YOU WILL NEED:
$1/2$ cup butter, softened
1 cup sugar
2 eggs
1 teaspoon vanilla extract
2 teaspoons baking powder

2 cups flour
Pinch of salt
1 cup milk
1 cup chocolate chips

Preheat oven to 375 degrees. Blend butter and sugar until fluffy. Beat in eggs. Add vanilla. In a separate bowl, mix together baking powder, flour, and salt. Add dry ingredients to the batter bit by bit, stirring constantly. Add milk. Stir in chocolate chips.

Grease and flour cupcake tins or use paper liners, and add batter until cups are two-thirds full. Bake for 20 to 25 minutes, then allow to cool before frosting.

Makes 20 to 24 cupcakes.

Moon Frosting

INGREDIENTS YOU WILL NEED:
1 cup heavy cream
$1/4$ cup powdered sugar
$1/4$ teaspoon vanilla

Whip all ingredients together and frost cooled cupcakes. Decorate with colored icing, writing things to celebrate about your first moon, using descriptive words such as *new, moon, mystery, magic, connections, changes, cool, sassy, moody,* and *growing up.*

KITCHEN SAFETY TIPS

Be sure to follow basic kitchen safety rules:

1. Check with your parents before starting a cooking project.

2. Get clean! Be sure to wash your hands. If you have long hair, tie it back.

3. Beware of germs: raw eggs, fish, and meat can contain harmful ones. Thoroughly wash cutting boards, knives, and other cooking utensils in hot, soapy water after each use. And don't eat raw dough that contains eggs, as you could get sick.

4. Ask for help until you're more experienced in the kitchen; adults can help out with knives and electrical appliances. Make sure an adult is around when you're lighting matches, dealing with a hot oven, or cooking on a range.

5. Be careful never to touch an electrical appliance when your hands are wet, as you could get an electric shock.

6. Make sure pot handles are turned in, toward the middle of the stove, and do not point out, toward the edge. Someone walking by could bump the handle and accidentally knock the pot off, scalding herself or someone else.

7. Use potholders to protect your hands from burns when placing something in the oven or taking it out.

8. Use a timer and remove cooked items promptly.

9. Stay close to things cooking on the stove, so that they don't boil over. Turn off the stove burners and oven when you are finished.

10. Clean up as you go. If you spill anything, clean it up immediately. It saves you from having to clean up a giant mess at the end, when all you really want to do is eat the goodies you've made.

Have fun! It feels so great to enjoy your cooking creations and to see other people enjoying them, too.

Moontime Magic

Celebrate your first moon by dressing up in beautiful clothes. Wear something with a moon on it, like a necklace or anklet. Draw a small crescent moon and star on your cheek, or paint moons on your finger nails.

For thousands of years, women from all over the world have recognized the special time of the first moon. As you grow from a girl into a young woman, your body, mind, and spirit will experience many astonishing changes. Throughout your life, you will continue to experience transition and change. If you treat yourself with extra care and ceremony during this first moon, it will give you strength and confidence throughout your life and during other times of change. Mark this time of your life with fun, happiness, love, and celebration.

chapter 3

REDEFINE PMS
Preparing Myself to Shine

*We need to learn how to nurture ourselves, each other,
and the planet. One way girls and women can begin to do
this is to just allow themselves some time, even an hour or two
each month, to do something that deeply nurtures them.*

— Shinan Barclay, author

Moontime Mythology: A Southern Ute Indian Moontime Story

long time ago, women did as they do now — they held the family.
They held the power (life force) of the family; they held its happiness
and joy; they held its sorrow and disappointments. As time passed, the
negative emotions and heartache that the women took upon themselves on behalf of their families began to weigh them down. The
women became sick and, finally, could no longer take on the burdens
of the family. Yet the Creator had given them the nature to do so.

One day, a woman was out in the forest, crying because the bur-
den had become so great, when Raven heard her and asked, "Mother,
why do you cry?"

The woman responded, "I love my family so very much. I hold my family in my heart and soul, but the pains of life have filled me up. I can no longer help my family. I can no longer take their burdens from them. I just don't know what to do."

Raven responded, "I understand the pain you feel, as I feel it also. I will go and ask Grandmother Ocean if she knows what to do." So Raven flew to the ocean and shared with Grandmother the plight of the women.

Grandmother Ocean responded, "If the women will come to me, I will wash their pain from them, but this won't help the ones who are far away. Let me ask my sister, Grandmother Moon, if she can help."

So Grandmother Ocean spoke to her sister of the women's plight. Grandmother Moon responded, "I am the power of the feminine. I will send your waters, carrying my power, into the women, my sisters. Once every moon cycle, you shall come into the women through me and purify them." And she did this.

So, ever since then, every woman has a time in each moon cycle when she embodies the power of the moon and the cleansing ocean flows through her. We call this the woman's time of the moon, or moontime.

What Is PMS?

Premenstrual syndrome (PMS) usually occurs at some point during the two weeks before the first day of your period. Symptoms can include feeling tired or grumpy or having mood swings; feeling bloated (a heavy or swollen feeling in your lower belly) and/or having tender breasts; or skin blemishes, acne, headaches, and cramping, as well as increased sensitivity to feelings, smells, and sounds. Some women never experience any of these symptoms, others experience a few symptoms, and still others experience all of them. There might also be other PMS experiences — not all of them negative — than those on this general list. It is not clear exactly what causes PMS. Certain foods and substances, such as caffeinated drinks (soda, coffee, tea), can contribute to PMS. Many women have also discovered that when they are especially stressed, they experience worse PMS. The best way to understand it, and to figure out what might trigger PMS in yourself, is to pay very close attention to your body, your feelings, and your outlook. Many women have found that when they change their attitudes about their moontime, looking at it as a time of renewal rather than a drag, their difficult PMS symptoms decrease and even disappear completely! It is often fulfilling to keep busy doing things you love to do, working and playing hard and being out in the world. But often our desire to keep going in the world keeps us from listening to our inner needs. PMS teaches women to balance *being* time and *doing* time.

Redefine PMS: Preparing Myself to Shine

Preparing: To make ready.
Myself: Me, the radiant being that I am.
Shine: To give out light, to be bright, to illuminate.

I used to have horrible PMS. I was grumpy and irritable, my skin broke out, I dropped things a lot, and I burst into tears at the simplest thing. It was as if all the emotions I had experienced during the weeks since my previous moontime, and all the worries I carried with me, came bubbling up to the surface at the same time, about four days before the start of my period. I would try to ignore and push through the PMS, knowing that my body's discomfort and my distress would pass and I would feel better soon, but the cycle repeated monthly, and with each month a new symptom appeared — cramps, headaches, fatigue, and irritability.

Then I heard some women talk about the special ways they treated themselves just before and/or during their moontime. I was reminded of my friend Tory's note from her nanny, in which she reminded Tory to take special care of herself. Listening to them, I learned how to make new nutritional and exercise choices to help me through PMS, and I learned how important it is for girls and women to take time just for themselves.

I decided give this stuff a try. Like I mentioned, I knew that my symptoms were at their worst about four days before my period, so I chose that as my "day off from the world" day. No chores, no work; just time for me. I take walks, write in my journal, draw, and pamper myself with bubble baths, homemade facials, yummy food, and hanging out. During my period, I try not to push myself so hard. I lighten up and relax more. I daydream a lot. Having this day to myself completely changed my life and my moontime experience.

My uncomfortable PMS symptoms are sometimes nonexistent now, and I feel great when my period arrives. My day off gives me time to feel rested, peaceful, and happy inside, so that by the third or fourth day of my period, I am ready to go out and shine in the world once more. It just wasn't natural to expect myself to feel energetic and extroverted all the time. When I thought that way, I became frustrated and irritable with myself and other people. Now I love my "down" days — days to just be quiet and introverted, days to enjoy my different moods. Down time also stimulates and revitalizes my creativity. By the time I am ready to go back into the world, I am full of brilliant and fun new ideas, dreams, and visions. I feel balanced and inspired.

Moontime Wisdom

Every moontime cycle offers an opportunity to redefine yourself. Each month, you can take a little time-out from the world, be it a few hours or a day. You can use this time to let go of things that aren't working in your life, celebrate things that you like about yourself, pamper and nourish yourself and your beauty, dream a new dream, and come out ready for the world in front of you.

The greatest thing about a monthly time-out is that not only your body but also nature's own cycles are completely in harmony with it. Nature has a built-in cycle of self-renewal that we can use to stay healthy, happy, and full of juicy good thoughts, energy, and inspiration. By observing the change of seasons, we see that in the winter, seeds lay in the darkness beneath Earth's surface, and once they are ready, they push up through the soil and grow beautiful flowers in the spring. In the summer sun they grow strong, and in the fall they die and their seeds return to the Earth to begin the cycle again. Just as in nature's changing seasons, each moontime cycle presents an opportunity to look within ourselves, grow quiet, listen, and emerge with renewed energy and vision.

A PMS Tool Kit: Get to Know, Love, and Decipher Your Moods

The days before moontime, when PMS usually occurs, are a perfect time to get to know more about yourself and your moods. Many girls and women find that this is a time when their feelings are easy to access because emotions are close to the surface. The following tools are part of my survival kit for moontime moods. I also added some ideas from other girls and women. Enjoy these tools, and create your own.

1. Create a moontime moods calendar. Included in this book's kit are mood stickers that you can use to easily track your different moods. Each day, pick out the sticker (or stickers) that best represents your feelings on that day, and put it on that day's date on a calendar. After a few months, you might notice a pattern starting to emerge: you might feel the same way on the same day of each month, and you can see if this is related to your cycle. You might notice similarities from month to month, or you might not. Try using the mood calendar for at least three months, and then see what similarities and patterns you notice.

2. Put your moods to work for you. Moontime can mean mood changes. And moods are the stuff that great art is made from. Draw your feelings; write down your most exaggerated and elaborate story about your dreams, worries, fears, and desires; or make beautiful art. Invite all your moods in. Get to know them. Then let them show you how to use them to bring your visions to life.

3. Remember that you are more than your emotions, even though some feelings can be very strong. They are here to show you something about yourself, but they are not *you*. You can feel them, and then you can let them go.

4. Remember the truth about feelings: no matter how you feel — happy, sad, mad, afraid, alone, confused, excited, frustrated, curious, jealous, spiteful — all feelings are okay, acceptable, and normal. How we relate to our feelings and what we do with them are another step. I felt so relieved when I learned this. I always had believed that if

I had what I thought was a "bad feeling," something terrible would happen, or I thought that I was terrible for having that feeling. Then I learned that all people have pretty much the same feelings — it's what we do with those feelings that defines what our lives are like and how we feel about ourselves.

5. Find at least one person you can share your most real self and feelings with. This might be a friend, parent, teacher, counselor, coach, sister, or aunt. Or you can invite a group of your friends together and create a *support circle*. Support circles can include your friends or anyone else you really like and trust, like your mom or your aunt. You can meet and talk together, sharing your feelings and experiences. Support circles are great because you hear lots of people's ideas and feelings in a safe and caring place.

When I was a young girl, I thought I had to do everything alone. If I made a mistake, I was scared that I would disappoint people who mattered to me, so I wouldn't talk to them about it. If I was mad at those closest to me, I felt guilty, so I wouldn't say I was mad. I also thought I had to keep things secret. This was no way to live! Luckily, I had sisters and friends I could turn to, people I knew would not judge me.

When I was eighteen, I learned about support circles where I could share my feelings in a safe and accepting group environment. The more I learned to trust other people and to tell them what was going on with me, and the less I worried about being judged, the more I liked to share my feelings. I learned I didn't have to figure out my life all on my own.

Now I call my trusted friends almost daily with any concerns that I want to let go of. I am amazed at how much sharing my thoughts and feelings with people I trust helps me to feel better inside and to make better choices in my life. You could invite your friends to join you in a support circle, a support chat room, or weekly phone check-ins to share your feelings, experiences, dreams, and visions.

6. Help someone else. Sometimes this is one of the best ways to deal with stress. Try a little service. Take care of a neighbor's garden, volunteer at a nursing home, or help out at an animal shelter. When you do something to improve your community, you also improve your feelings about yourself.

7. When you feel sad, write in your journal, sing the blues, draw how you feel, take a walk, call a friend, hug a tree, or read poetry.

8. When you feel mad, give yourself permission to let all your anger out in a safe and creative way. You might feel like screaming into your pillow, banging on a drum, punching a punching bag, or asking a friend if she or he will listen to you. Anger can be a powerful force, creating changes in our lives. It is destructive only when it is directed at ourselves or others in a hurtful way. You can express anger without harm in your journal, in song, in a dance, in sports, or in a play.

9. When you feel lonely, write a letter to yourself. Write everything that you long to hear from someone you love. Put it in an envelope, stamp it, and send it to yourself. Remember that even though you might feel lonely, you

are never really alone. We are all connected by love — even if we can't always see it.

10. Support yourself by spending quality time alone. If you have a good relationship with yourself, you will know how to handle anything that life brings your way. You will know how to follow your heart.

I learned about a saying that can help anybody in times of stress. It goes like this: HALT! Don't get too (H) hungry, (A) angry, (L) lonely, or (T) tired.

If you feel hungry, eat, even if it is just a little. This will keep your emotions steadier during your moontime. If you are angry, pause, take a breath, and call a friend to talk it out. If you are lonely, start a project that includes your favorite things in life — like making a scrapbook or decorating your bedroom wall. If you are tired, give yourself a break and take a nap. It is important, especially at your moontime, to support yourself by checking in on what you need.

Moontime Herstory: Frida Kahlo

I never painted my dreams. I painted my own reality.

— Frida Kahlo, artist

Frida Kahlo is known for her vibrant and fiery spirit and her love for and dedication to painting. (*Frida*, a 2002 movie about her life starring Salma Hayek, won Academy Awards.) Born in Mexico City to a Hungarian-Jewish father and a Catholic mother of Spanish and Native American descent, Kahlo survived polio to become a fearless

your sassy self and see what kind of creative and inspiring stuff you can cook up. You might even be inspired to try out variations of this recipe and adjust it just to your perfect liking. Preparation time is about 40 minutes.

INGREDIENTS YOU WILL NEED:
1 six-ounce jar marinated artichoke hearts
1 cup chopped broccoli florets
1 cup chopped onion
1 stalk celery, minced
2 teaspoons salt
2 purple potatoes, scrubbed and thinly sliced
4 medium cloves garlic, minced
1 teaspoon dried basil
4 cups water
$^1/_2$ pound spinach, minced (or 10 ounces frozen chopped spinach, defrosted and drained)
2 tablespoons fresh lemon juice
Freshly ground black pepper to taste
1 cup peas (fresh or frozen)
Minced fresh parsley to taste

Drain the liquid from the marinated artichoke hearts into a soup pot. Chop hearts coarsely and set aside. Gently heat artichoke liquid.

Add chopped onion to artichoke liquid and sauté over medium heat for 5 minutes.

Add broccoli, celery, salt, potatoes, garlic, and basil. Sauté for 10 minutes over low heat, stirring occasionally.

Add water and bring to a boil. Stir, cover, and let simmer 15 to 20 minutes, until potatoes are tender.

Add artichoke hearts and spinach. Cover and cook over low heat another 5 minutes. Set aside until just before serving time.

Begin heating the soup about 10 minutes before serving. When it is hot, stir in lemon juice, black pepper, and peas. Allow to cook for a few more minutes, then serve topped with freshly minced parsley.

Serves 6. Yum!

Mystical Muffins

There is nothing better than the smell of freshly baked corn muffins wafting through the house when all I want to do is wrap myself up in a blanket and lie on the couch with a great book and a cup of raspberry tea. These muffins take about 10 minutes to prepare and 15 to 20 minutes to bake. You will need a muffin pan.

INGREDIENTS YOU WILL NEED:
1 $1/2$ cups unbleached white flour
$1/2$ teaspoon baking soda
2 teaspoons baking powder
$1/2$ teaspoon salt
1 cup yellow cornmeal
1 $1/2$ cups milk
1 egg
5 tablespoons melted butter
4 tablespoons dark molasses
3 tablespoons sugar
Dash of cinnamon

Preheat oven to 375 degrees. Lightly grease 12 muffin cups, unless they're nonstick.

Cooling Cucumber Toner

INGREDIENTS YOU WILL NEED:
$1/2$ cucumber, unpeeled
3 teaspoons witch hazel
1 teaspoon mineral water or lavender water

Place cucumber in a blender and pulp it. Add witch hazel and water, then strain through a sieve. Set aside pulp. Dip a cotton ball in the liquid mixture and dab on your face. Refrigerate the leftovers. (Any recipes with fresh fruit or vegetables must be used within three days.) Follow with your favorite oil-free moisturizer. Notice how your skin tingles and glows!

Mini-Moontime PMS Meditation

Find a place to sit or lie down and relax. Close your eyes. Take a few deep breaths.

Notice how your body feels. Where is it relaxed? What does that feel like? Where is it tense or uncomfortable? What does that feel like?

Let your breath travel to the tense places. As you breathe in, let the breath gently relieve the tension. Imagine any worries or fears leaving your body with your exhalation. As you inhale, imagine breathing in warm golden light. Allow the warm light to travel through your whole body, especially to any cramped or blocked areas.

See the light dissolving any blocks, allowing energy to move freely through your body. See and feel your body relaxed, healthy, and vibrant. When you feel this meditation is complete, open your eyes.

Moontime Magic

Draw a picture of a butterfly. Growing from a caterpillar to a winged creature, the butterfly is nature's expert on the art of transformation! Pretend your butterfly is carrying your worries away.

Moontime Journaling: Preparing Myself to Shine

Take out your moontime journal. Write about what your perfect self-care day would include. Consider your list a reminder to treat yourself with gentleness each month. Here is a sample list of simple things you can do:

Stay in bed longer.
Take walks.
Eat delicious, healthy food.
Paint your nails.
Write poetry.
Daydream.
Give yourself a facial.
Take a bubble bath.
Meditate.
Just be.

If you indulge in self-care and pampering during your moontime, you will find yourself looking forward to your cycle each month, and you will truly redefine PMS by preparing yourself to shine!

To me, being a girl and becoming a woman mean that I am blessed with the power and magic of creativity and that I am connected to nature. Having a female body means that I have a menstrual cycle, and that cycle connects me in a very physical way to nature's larger cycles. Nature's cycles are perfectly balanced. This means that if I carefully pay attention to the natural rhythms and cycles of my body, the dreams in my heart, and the ideas in my head, I can do anything I dream of doing, because I have a built-in natural system of balance and support. My definition of being a girl (and now a woman) is that I am fun, creative, strong, assertive, shy, silly, beautiful, interesting, powerful, feminine, tough, smart, energetic, outgoing, reserved, and everything in between. I am myself. Being a woman means I am free to be full of contradictions and to embrace the individuality that makes me *me*. Being a woman means that I am love, grace, and beauty in motion. I am magical and amazing. I am connected to all life. I have the power to create.

Many things can influence your definition of a girl, and your definition of yourself as a girl. The way you think of yourself and what you learn from your family, friends, school and community, country, the media, and history all shape your definition. I have found that defining what it means to be a woman for myself is important because it gives me the power to influence how the world defines me. I won't settle for any external definition of myself — I define myself first, and I continue to redefine myself as I grow and change throughout my life. Self-definition is important for every girl and woman.

How do you do this? I first acknowledge my female body and its rhythms; then my personal interests, talents, and desires; and then my personal history, my ancestral history, and women's history. Acknowledging all these aspects of myself gives me the opportunity to shape and dream my own future because I know that I carry many experiences within myself. This knowledge gives me strength and carries me forward. I like finding role models, too, among girls and women I admire. This helps me to expand my views and my beliefs and to imagine the possibilities of what it means to be a girl or a woman.

Moontime Mythology

This passage is from the book *Flowering Woman: Moontime for Kory,* by Shinan Barclay and Mary Dillon.

"The Great Mother Goddess has blessed women," whispered Chalice, the Grand Mother of the West. "She has given us our moontime. Our moontime is for renewal, for nourishing our inner strength, for getting in touch with our deepest feelings and for expressing our power. This special time is to re-attune to our own personal rhythm so we can begin our cycle again pure and strong. It is the time when the Goddess is most likely to use each woman as a channel to pour out her truth and beauty in the form of songs, poems, stories, new ideas and new ideals. Guard this special time of your moon. Don't make yourself so busy that you have no time to do the work of the Goddess. Because she brings a special blessing for us all."

to do and how she likes to play. Imagine all the love in the world flowing toward her.

Now see this young girl growing older still. Notice that her body is beginning to change shape. Place your hands on your belly. Take a few minutes to notice your own body now. Think about your life today. See yourself with your friends, and think about what makes you happy. See yourself nourishing your body with healthy, good food. Imagine moving your body in play, sports, or dance. Notice how you feel in your body. Think about what interests you most in the world. What are your dreams? How does it feel to be you today? Now feel all the love in the world flow into your own body. Your body becomes warm from head to toe, surrounded with love and support.

Finally, imagine looking into the future, a few years from now. See how your body has changed and grown even more. See how comfortable you are in your body; notice the smile on your face. See how your future self loves her life. Imagine all the love in the world flowing toward her. In your imagination, ask your future self if she has any advice that might help you as you grow during the next few years. Listen gently to what she says.

When you are ready, ease your attention back to today. Open your eyes and come out of the meditation. You might want to stay centered and write about your experience. Or you might want to share it with someone. Pay attention to the lessons you taught yourself, and honor the feelings you experienced.

Moontime Journaling

Find a place to hang out and take out your moontime journal. Complete the following sentences:

Being a girl means . . .

What I like most about being a girl is . . .

The hardest part about being a girl is . . .

My mom thinks girls are . . .

My dad thinks girls are . . .

Images of girls I see on TV or in magazines make me think that being a girl means . . .

I think girls are . . .

A girl I really admire is . . . , because she . . .

A woman I really admire is . . . , because she . . .

Moontime Magic:
Scented Bubble Bath

Treat yourself to a magical moontime bath! Add twelve drops of your favorite essential oils or bath gel to the tub under running water. Turn off the lights and (with permission) light a candle. Luxuriate in your bubble bath while letting your mind wander.

Moontime Moments:
Adorn Yourself with Jewels

Create a piece of beautiful moontime jewelry, put it on, and feel how beautiful and magical you are!

How to Bead a Necklace

SUPPLIES YOU WILL NEED:
Necklace wire or fishing line
Scissors or pliers
A set of necklace clasps
Your favorite beads, in any shape, size, or color

If you do not have these items at home, you can find them at any crafts store or bead shop. For a special touch, include one or two extra-fancy charm beads, such as a moon, butterfly, heart, or your initial.

First, carefully cut the fishing line or necklace wire to the length that you need. You might want to make a long necklace, a short necklace, or maybe a bracelet or anklet. Be careful when measuring, and be sure to leave an extra 6 inches so that you can easily attach the clasps at the end of your beading. (If you make a long necklace, you won't need to use clasps, as you can just fit the necklace over your head, so you could even use ribbon, yarn, twine, or other materials instead of wire or line.)

Tie a knot in one end of the wire or line and attach one of the clasps to it. Leave 2 to 3 inches of wire or line at the end, below the clasp and knot. Make sure the knot and clasp are large enough that the beads will not slip over them and fall off when you string them.

Now you can start beading. Use your imagination: you can create patterns or use beads in your favorite colors. You can use different sizes or combinations of beads. This is your special, beautiful beading creation.

Once you are finished beading, tie a knot at the other end of the line. Make sure it is secure so that you can easily attach the other necklace clasp. Then cut off the extra wire or line on both ends. Wear it with pride!

As you grow from a girl into a woman, think about the kind of woman you aspire to be. Choose role models who display qualities you admire. You can ask yourself how you think your role model might handle a certain situation that you are dealing with. If you aspire to be a great athlete, perhaps you think of Mia Hamm, or Serena or Venus Williams. If you aspire to be a poet, perhaps you think of Maya Angelou. Role models help broaden our definition of ourselves and fill our lives with possibility.

Remember to define yourself on your terms first and that as you do, you will influence a positive definition for other girls and women in the world.

chapter 5

BODY CHANGES

Like the seed within the flower, like the flower within the seed,
the hidden things will be revealed, if you believe, if you believe.

— Kelli Selah, singer

Your body changes every moment of every day. We are always in transition, whether we notice it or not. We experience transitions many times each day — the day turns to night and then to day again; we move from our home life to our school life, from friend time to family time. We experience transitions over the years, too, as we move from being children to teenagers to adults. Change is a constant in our lives. It is reflected in the seasons, too. Sometimes it feels great, and sometimes it feels awful. Accepting that life is full of transformations, and learning about specific changes, helps you to find creative ways to be a *part* of all this change, rather than feeling that change just happens to you.

Enjoying and getting to know your changing body are important because the body is powerful, amazing, and capable of so many incredible things. As you are already aware, your body's changes might be different from those of other girls' and women's bodies. But we all undergo most of the changes I describe below.

Your skin will go through a change as you turn from a girl into a woman: it might be oilier or prone to breakouts sometimes. Or it might get drier. The main change you will notice is that your skin will just need a little more care than it did when you were younger.

Your breasts will develop and grow fuller, and you will need to wear comfortable underclothes — bras and exercise bras — for support. Your hips might widen. Your body will grow hair in new places — on your pubic (genital) area and under your arms. The hair on your legs might grow and become darker. All these changes are normal, expected, and part of growing up.

When I first noticed my body changing, I was about eleven years old. My best friend and I talked about body changes a lot. One night she slept over, and in the bathroom she showed me the first signs of her pubic hair. We both screamed and laughed. I felt excited about my body changing, but kind of nervous, too. When I was twelve, my breasts began to develop, and my mom bought me a bra. In those days, it was called a training bra. (I know: lame name!)

Some of my friends were already much more developed than I was. I wasn't sure how I felt about that. I wanted to stay a kid, with my kid's body, and not worry about bras and periods and what my body looked like compared to my friends'. I was also excited about my body changing, and I liked dressing up in my older sisters' clothes. I liked looking in the mirror and imagining how I might look in a few more years.

But it was those in-between years that were the hardest. I felt like I had no control over anything happening to my body. I was growing taller but not wider, so I was super-scrawny, with bony knees. My skin started getting pimples. My feet were too big for the rest of me, and I was very clumsy for a while. I tried to make up for that by getting a new hairstyle. I wanted that long, wavy, pretty hair that some of the actresses I saw on TV had. I ended up getting a really bad perm that frizzed my straight blond hair. Then I had to get braces as well. I felt very freakish. Mostly, I wanted to find a cocoon to hide in until this whole transformation thing had happened. I wanted a lot of privacy and felt incredibly self-conscious and exposed at the slightest comment about me or my appearance.

The hardest part was that I thought that other people saw me in the horrible and awkward way I was starting to see myself — and the truth is, they didn't at all. At this point, I think, I mentally separated myself from the changes in my body because they seemed way too uncomfortable. I just tried to ignore the changes that were happening or to pretend I didn't notice them.

Another uncomfortable change was the new attention my friends and I received from other people. My very embarrassing aunt exclaimed in front of the whole family, "Oh, you are starting to blossom! Look at those breasts!" I really wanted to shrink away. I noticed how the boys in my school paid a lot of attention to the more developed girls, and I wondered if I would ever develop as they had. It was all just so unknown. And I dreaded the occasional gross stares from older men on the street. It seemed that so many changes were taking place at once. Some were great, but many just upset me.

By the age of fifteen, most of the changes had happened, and believe it or not, I loved my new body. I loved the way my clothes fit my new curves and how strong my growing body felt. But there were some rough times. The most helpful thing I did was talk to my friends about those times, and I realized that we were all in this growing-up thing together. Sharing our nightmare moments, like my aunt's totally weird comment, made us laugh for hours. Really, I don't think there is anything better than laughing with friends about all the oddness we experience as our bodies shift and we try to catch up with them.

"MY CHANGING BODY," BY LIZZY, AGE SIXTEEN

It's one of those things that just make you want to close your eyes and wake up when they're all over. At first it's like, "Dear God, please help me out of this awkward stage! Let me open my eyes and be a woman!" But after a while — I can't explain it — I suddenly took a deep breath and realized it's not that bad. It's like you blink and suddenly you are comfortable in your own skin, excited and almost breathless at the inner workings of your own body. I could let go of my sadness at feeling like a door had closed, and realize that maybe new doors were opening. I am part of all women, connected by Mother Earth's cycle. To me, my period is magical now; I feel blessed to be in this body, so blessed to have been a girl and so excited to become a woman.

A First Moon Celebration Story

Laura's parents are from Israel and have been living in the United States for the past thirteen years. This year, they were concerned about Laura because she was diagnosed with spinal scoliosis and had to have surgery to help correct it. Spinal scoliosis creates a curve in the spine that can become worse over time. The surgeons fused parts of her spine together and inserted metal rods and screws in her back to keep it straight. The whole ordeal lasted several months and included many days of painful recovery and physical therapy. Laura lost ten pounds, which her parents feared would delay her first moon. They knew not only that the onset of menstruation would welcome Laura into her womanhood, but also that the hormonal changes in her body would slow down the scoliosis's growth.

Now Laura is in eighth grade and has just had her first moon. Laura's entire family celebrated. Her mother, father, and brother danced and called their relatives in Israel with the news so that they too could join the celebration. This summer, Laura and her mom will take a trip to France together to celebrate her arrival into womanhood.

Moontime Mythology: Rosh Chodesh

Women and the moon have long been linked in many traditions and religions. Rosh Chodesh, the Jewish new moon festival, is traditionally recognized as a women's holiday. A marker of the new month (the Hebrew calendar is based on the moon), Rosh Chodesh is God's reward to women.

Growing-Up Advice for Girls, from Girls and Women Fifteen to Fifty

Grow into and get to know your new and changing body through dance or sports.

Be in your body.

Give yourself all the privacy you want to create a cocoon, and while you're in it pay more attention to your inner self or write or paint about what you are going through.

Be a witness to your own growth.

Touch and view your body; get to know it!

Write poetry.

Hang out with fun, supportive girls. Host a girls' circle and support one another.

Go out for team sports.

Journal.

Learn about all the cool changes your body is going through.

Remember that even though some girls don't show it, all of us go through this passage, and it ain't always easy!

Talk about your changes and feelings with your mom or a trusted older woman friend.

You are the only *you* here. Only you can bring the gifts of who you are to the world.

Stay true and honest, and you can handle anything!

Sometimes the bad stuff turns out to be good.

You are enough just as you are!

Remember, all those girls in magazines are airbrushed. They're not real!

It can be fun to wear revealing clothes and to celebrate your body. But, unfortunately, we live in a world where not all people feel the same way. Be aware that what you wear attracts attention, and some of it you might not want. Choose your clothes with care and awareness so that you always honor yourself!

Surround yourself with people who respect you and treat you well.

Your body is beautiful, strong, and healthy. Each body has its own cycle, rhythm, size, and shape. Each body is a beautiful work of art.

Bodies in Motion

Being happy and comfortable in your body and with its changes has a lot to do with how your body feels.

Does your body feel strong and healthy to you? Do you feel fit? Exercise is an important part of caring for your changing body. It also helps to promote a healthy menstrual cycle and reduces PMS symptoms, including cramping. What do you like to do for exercise? Take walks? Dance? Play sports? Everybody is different, and some types of exercise might be a better fit for you than others. For example, my goddaughter Lizzy loves long-distance running but cannot stand being in a gym. My niece Fran loves to hike and rock climb. Jen loves to walk. Kelli dances hip-hop for hours. Finding out what you love to do and making it a part of your life are among the best things you can do for your body and your health.

Exercise releases natural chemicals called *endorphins* in your body that actually make you feel good. I love running long distances. I don't like running really fast, but I do like slow, long runs on mountain trails. They give me time to be out in nature and to unwind from all the events of my day. Out on the trails, it is just me and the sound of my feet carrying me on the path. Sometimes I talk out loud to the trees — or the flowers and rocks

— around me; sometimes I just talk in my head. I like to have conversations with nature about everything going on in my life and to ask for answers or solutions to problems I am having. By the end of my run, my head is always clear and answers are easy to find.

I've discovered another good thing about running (and other individual sports): every time I make it on a long run, it adds to my confidence in my ability to make it or come through in other areas of my life. Whenever I feel a crisis of confidence, I go for a run. Feeling the strength of my muscles and the way my body can move across the land reminds me that I am strong — inside and out — and that I can handle whatever challenges face me. Running not only makes my body even stronger, it also builds the strength of my mind and confidence.

KEEPING IT BALANCED

Whatever you do for exercise, remember to listen to your body and to do what feels good. When it is time to play, play. When it is time to rest, let yourself rest. It's important to keep your nutrition, exercise, and rest time in balance.

Sometimes athletes, especially those with a very low body-fat percentage, such as gymnasts or long-distance runners (who have to put in hours of workout daily and adhere to a strict eating plan), may have late puberty or may stop getting their period. This is called *female athletic syndrome* (FAS). Once a young woman cuts back on exercising and gains some body fat, her period will resume. However, prolonged FAS can lead to bone damage and other problems like osteoporosis (weak bones) later in life. If you miss your period more than three times and if your weight is low, check in with your doctor.

Mini-Moontime Meditation:
Thanking Your Body

Find a comfortable place to sit or lie down and relax. Take a few deep breaths, and let yourself relax more with each exhalation. See your body in your mind's eye, and take a little time to check in on it.

Place attention on each area of your body, starting with your head. Let your hands move to each area and rest there as you say "hi" to it.

As you see and feel your head, thank it for all the thinking it does each day. Thank your hair for its warmth and for the way it feels when a breeze blows it against your skin. Thank your eyes for showing you the beauty of the world. Thank your ears for the music they let you hear. Thank your nose for introducing you to the sweet scents of flowers. Thank your mouth for letting you enjoy delicious foods. Thank your throat for singing and speaking.

Now thank your arms for hugging. Thank your hands for touching. Thank your heart for loving. Thank your skin for feeling the warmth of the sun as well as the chill of the wind. Thank your belly for being your center, for balancing you as you move in the world. Thank your womb for bleeding, for connecting you to the greater cycles of life. Thank your legs for walking and letting you stand. Thank your feet for taking you where you want to go.

Now take a few moments to breathe into your whole body, and thank your breath for breathing you into life each moment. When you are ready, open your eyes, enjoying your body and your senses and the gifts they are.

Moontime Journaling

Take out your moontime journal. Write about how you felt during this moontime meditation. What do you like about your body? What gifts does your body give you?

Moontime Magic: Create Your Own Magical Mist

Flower essences and essential oils are wonderful healing gifts from the Earth. Flower essences are extracts that carry the energetic imprint, or personality, of the flower but have no scent. Essential oils, which are used in aromatherapy, are oils extracted from flowers, and each carries a unique scent that promotes physical, emotional, and spiritual health. Every flower essence and essential oil has its own personality; no two are alike. Flowers are amazing healers.

Flower essences and essential oils work wonderfully together. You can combine them to use in your bath or as a pillow spray. You can use them for help with fears and moods, for creative inspiration, for healing, to ease physical pain, and for skin and body care. It's fun to create your own mixtures and to create them as gifts for friends.

You can purchase flower essences, essential oils, and spray bottles at health food stores or order them online. Before you buy, it's a good idea to decide which flower essences you want by reading about them in books or online. (I have included my favorite suppliers in the resources section at the back of this book.) Remember that flower essences have no scent, so you will select them based on their special healing gifts. Take a trip to your local health food store or specialty shop and give yourself time to sample the scents of various essential oils. Be sure to ask the retail professionals any and all questions you might have about the products they are selling. Once you have decided on a couple you like, you might want to read about which healing qualities these oils have. Trust yourself on the ones you want to use. There is no "right way" to choose an essential oil for yourself. Just have fun and pick out what you like.

Magical Mist

SUPPLIES YOU WILL NEED:
Clean empty spray bottle (I like the pretty blue ones)
4 ounces spring water (bottled water is great)
Your favorite essential oil(s)
Your favorite flower essence(s)

Before you begin, it can be fun to decorate your bottle with stickers, ribbons, metallic ink, or any other wonderful touches.

Take off the spray cap and fill bottle with spring water. Place 6 drops of each essential oil in the water.

If you like that combination, next add 8 drops of each flower essence to the oil-water mixture. Put the spray cap back on tightly. Shake well for about 20 seconds. Now mist yourself. Do you like it? Keep experimenting to create an array of personal mists.

Glow-Girl Floral Moontime Mist

Following are suggestions for a mist of essential oils and flower essences that might be helpful for you around your moontime. This mist smells and feels divine, and it is my all-time favorite.

SUPPLIES YOU WILL NEED:
6 drops rose essential oil
3 drops roman chamomile essential oil
2 drops pomegranate flower essence
2 drops alpine lily flower essence
2 drops chamomile flower essence

Repeat the Magical Mist directions. Fill a clean spray bottle with 4 ounces spring water. Add essential oils and flower essences. Replace spray cap and shake well.

Rose oil is calming and emotionally healing. It can also be worn as perfume. Roman chamomile oil is calming and helps to balance emotions. Pomegranate flower essence promotes a healthy attitude toward the start of menstruation and balances the forces of creativity. Alpine lily essence helps to promote a healthy relationship with menstruation and body development. It helps to harmonize your feelings about your female body with the emotions and feelings in your heart. Chamomile flower essence helps with mood swings and balances emotions.

Have fun trying out new scents and essences. When you have created your own misting spray, you can spray it directly on yourself or around your room, or use it on your pillow at night to give yourself sweet dreams.

Moontime Moments: You Are Beautiful

Look in the mirror and say to yourself, "I am beautiful, and I love my body!" Do this every time you see your reflection. Seeing your own beauty helps to keep it alive. See the beauty of others, too — your ability to do so is a reflection of the beauty within yourself.

chapter 6

BODY WISDOM

Your body has great wisdom; let it show that wisdom to you! When treated with care, your body is your greatest friend. It can tell you everything you need to know.

Moontime Herstory: Moontime and the Origins of Healing

Some of the most ancient human artifacts discovered are about thirty-seven thousand years old. They are small statues of female humans who were believed to be the guardians of the Earth. The statues were used to remind people of the mysterious power of the female to create and care for life on Earth.

Since the beginning of time, women have been great healers, and they have learned to heal by listening to and caring for their bodies. Early observation of the menstrual/lunar cycle helped women to develop healing skills. Observation of this cycle also helped people to develop time measurements, numbers, and calendars!

Learning to take care of your body is a central part of women's wisdom and can lead to all kinds of wonderful discoveries.

Trusting Your Body Wisdom

Listening to and accepting your body and the messages it sends you is the surest path to a healthy, beautiful body. By becoming quiet and listening to yourself, you can quite easily discover how to best care for yourself. Health is the natural harmony and balance that arise within the body and spirit when they are properly cared for, and all it requires is your willingness to listen. Some days, perfect health might mean eating a lot and resting. Other days, perfect health might mean active exercise and laughter.

Body Wisdom and Intuition

Besides telling you all you need to know about how to take care of your physical needs, listening to your body also gives you all the information you need to take care of yourself in any situation. This skill is called *intuition*. I like to think of my intuition as the part of myself that is always awake and paying attention, even if I am sleeping or distracted. My intuition is my own personal antenna.

The more you pay attention to the messages that intuition sends you, the sharper or finer-tuned your antenna becomes. For example, when some people are in an unsafe situation, they experience intuition as a queasy feeling in their stomachs that tells them it's time to leave. Intuition is the part of themselves that tells them that, even though everything might look okay on the outside, something isn't right about a person or a situation.

Your intuition can clue you in as to whether someone is being honest with you. It can also guide you to try out a new class or sport by giving you a little nudge from within, a little excitement at the idea of trying something new. And intuition can even help you be "lucky": sometimes, when something that seems lucky happens — for example, you're in the right place at the right time — you can look back and remember little messages or feelings you experienced that urged you to be there. That's intuition, and it is invaluable. It is your own personal bodyguard and dream maker. It is your personal healer and friend. If you learn to listen to your body and give yourself time for quiet, you will be able to develop a very strong understanding of your intuition and how it works. And by following your intuition, you will always be able to make good choices for yourself.

Trust yourself! Listen to your body and its desire for movement, dance, play, and sports. Take time to just chill. Hang out, sit, stretch, walk, read, and cry if you need to. The body is the physical expression of the spirit, so by doing what your body wants you to do, you can come to know your spirit. As you grow and express your beautiful self in ways that you love, your body grows stronger and healthier, and your spirit shines more and more.

Mini-Moontime Meditation: Listening to Your Body

Find a comfortable place to relax, lying down or sitting in a chair. Let your eyes close, and take a few deep breaths.

Tighten all the muscles in your body as much as you can, then release them all and exhale. Do this again. Notice how your body feels resting on the ground or in the chair. Are you comfortable? Do you need to adjust yourself to find a better position? If so, do that now. Feel your breath rising and falling in your chest. See the breath travel through your body, nourishing all your cells, massaging and relaxing your muscles.

Using your mind's eye, scan through your body. Are there any tight or tense areas? If so, bring your attention there and focus your breath into these areas. Take several breaths until the tightness has released.

When you are relaxed, ask yourself, "What does my body need from me today?" Placing your hands on your belly and breathing in, listen for your body's response.

When you feel your meditation is complete, begin to wiggle your toes and come out of your meditation, ready to respond to your body's needs.

Moontime Journaling

Take out your moontime journal. Write about your meditation. How did/does your body feel? Were you able to release any tightness through your breath? What messages did your body have for you today? Write them down. What can you do today to respond to your body's needs and be your own healer? Write down your plans.

Moontime Massage

Massage is a great way to prevent and relieve pain, balance emotions, and help you feel healthy. *Acupressure* is a type of massage that places pressure on certain points on the body, called *acupressure points,* to assist in healing. Acupressure points are special points that correspond to the various muscles and organs and to your energy. It is perfectly safe to use acupressure on yourself or someone else. Just pay attention to what feels good so that you don't press too hard, which *won't* feel good! Here are three acupressure massage techniques to try, the first for menstrual pain, the second for balancing the emotions of PMS, and the third for an excellent massage at any point during your moontime.

point 1

point 1

point 2

point 1

point 2

point 3

MENSTRUAL PAIN POINTS   PMS PAIN POINTS

MASSAGE FOR MENSTRUAL PAIN

Several acupressure points are important for this massage. The first pair of points is on the back at waist level, in the muscle bands beside the spine. The next single point is on the stomach, directly below the navel and in line with it. Point three is on the lower legs: it is at the base of both calf muscles, on the inside of the calves beside the shinbone. (Don't press these points on a pregnant person, as that can bring on bleeding). The last pair is on the front of the body, on the lower edges of the pelvic bones.

A good beginning is simply to hold your hand over the general area of one of these points. Let it rest there while you take a deep, relaxed breath. Then, using your fingertip, press gently on the point. Move your finger around the area, continuing to press gently until you feel a slight dip that tells you that you've reached the exact point. Press it lightly, holding the point until you feel the tissues underneath your fingertip soften and relax. Then slowly press into the point.

When a point is released — meaning freed up — and energy is running freely through it (which relieves any discomfort), you will know it by the slight pulsing or heartbeat that begins under your fingertip. This pulsing takes some experience to recognize. Hold most points for a couple of minutes.

PMS MASSAGE FOR EMOTIONAL RELIEF

The first pair of points for this massage is under the collarbone, where that bone meets the shoulder joints. Massage with small circular motions until you feel your body relax. Another good spot is on the little-finger sides of each wrist, in the hollow of the wrist joints. Again, gently massage each spot with small circular motions. As you do so, you can play sweet music and think nice thoughts for yourself.

MOONTIME MONTHLY MASSAGE

For an easy do-it-yourself massage that feels wonderful, rub six drops of essential oil or massage oil onto your lower stomach. Continue rubbing in a circular clockwise motion for several minutes to ease pressure and relieve cramping. Then let yourself drift off to a dreamy sleep.

MASSAGE WITH FRIENDS

You can do massage with your friends. Use massage oil and take turns giving one another foot rubs and pedicures. There are acupressure points above the heel and just below the anklebone, and rubbing these can be very soothing at moontime.

Moontime Magic: Body Art

Celebrate your body with body art. You might like to experiment with henna tattoos or temporary body paints. They are colorful, temporary, and perfectly safe. Maybe you will want to paint a moon and star on your ankle or a butterfly on your wrist.

For centuries, women's healing and body wisdom came from observing a woman's menstrual cycle. Paying attention to your own cycle, and what makes you feel good, will support you to be in good health throughout your life. Listening to your body's needs and responding will also strengthen your intuition. Following your intuition will help you be healthy, safe, and confident.

chapter 7

BODY IMAGE
How Our Self-Image Helps to
Create Our World

*I'm not the average girl from the video, and I'm not
built like a supermodel, but I've learned to love
myself unconditionally because I am a queen.*

— India Arie, "Video"

I love my body. I love how strong and healthy it is and how it carries me through my life. I love my eyes. They are big and blue and can see forever. I like my hair. It is blond and shiny, and I can wear it up or down, straight or curly. I like the way it feels on my skin in a breeze. I think I have a very special nose: sometimes I think it is unique and kind of Romanesque; other times I think it is pointy, like a fairy-tale witch's. But my nose lets me enjoy the amazing scents of roses and jasmine in the garden and the deliciousness of fresh bread baking in the oven. I like my lips and my mouth, for with them I can kiss and I can talk. I like my shape, the curves of my breasts and hips. I like my belly button. I like being ticklish. I love the feeling of wrapping myself up in a warm towel when I'm fresh out of the shower, and resting in that clean, warm, skin-tingling sensation. Bodies are amazing.

When I was eleven, I didn't like my body very much. I didn't like my forehead, my knees, my wrists, or my nose. I wanted to hide all these parts of myself all the time. One day, my friend commented that I had a big forehead, and from that day onward I always wore bangs. Even when I swam, I was so self-conscious about my forehead that I would pull my wet hair down to hide it, which made everyone laugh.

A few years later, another friend said, "You would be so pretty if only you got a nose job!" After that, I became totally obsessed with getting a nose job. I even visited a plastic surgeon to discuss it. He greatly discouraged me and said that I had a "delicate nose" that was in fact unique and Romanesque and that he thought it perfectly suited the rest of my face.

I spent many years trying to become like a girl in a magazine. I truly believed that if my nose were smaller or my body thinner or if I had better skin, I would be really great and have a perfect life, and everyone would love me. While trying so hard to be the image of perfection that I saw in all the magazines, I lost many chances to enjoy myself, my friends, school, and work. I lost out on learning to listen to and appreciate my body. Trying to make myself into some outer idea of beauty or perfection left me feeling pretty hopeless and somewhat empty.

I think my "ah ha" moment came when I learned that all girls, no matter what they look like, have the same fears and worries about themselves. Most girls also spend more time and money than they want to as they try to look like the images in magazines and movies, which girls imagine they should resemble. But in fact, even the girls in magazines have these worries and fears!

I noticed that the girls who seemed happiest to me were the ones who were really into something they loved. Observing them,

I decided to try something different. I decided to keep enjoying the fun stuff about beauty — like dressing in clothes that I loved and that made me feel good and taking good care of myself by eating right and exercising. *But,* I also decided to lose the worry and negative self-talk. I decided to focus my energy on things that I really liked and was interested in — like training for a marathon, reading books (fiction and nonfiction) about women I loved and admired, acting, and learning about the environment. Doing these things was what really changed my self-image and made me happy. Through this process, I learned that I have no control over how the world views me — no matter how "perfect" (or not) I look. I also learned that I needed to start being a lot nicer to myself. I cannot depend on the world to be nice, and I cannot depend on what the world defines as "beauty," but I *can* define beauty for myself — and that makes an impression on the world around me.

And by the way, today my boyfriend is always trying to push my bangs off my face and says I have the most beautiful face and fore-head ever, and he doesn't want me to hide them.

Moontime Herstory: Truly Beautiful Women

The beautiful woman is the one who really knows herself and makes the most out of everything she's got.

— Eileen Ford, entrepreneur

Reality is the world as you feel it to be, as you wish it into being.

— Diana Vreeland, former editor of
Harper's Bazaar and *Vogue* magazines

Diana Vreeland grew up in New York and Paris in the early 1900s. Her beautiful and high-society mother told her that her lack-luster looks would bring her rejection in life, especially by high society. Not one to let life pass her by, Diana decided to redefine herself by re-creating every aspect of herself and taking the focus off her looks. She read hungrily, became a graceful dancer, studied fashion and makeup, and developed exquisite poise. It worked. She married the handsome Reed Vreeland, and when she was twenty she became a bigger socialite than her mother, traveling around the world with her international friends.

More important, when she was picked to be an editor for *Harper's Bazaar*, she used her gift for self-transformation to reinvent the fashion magazine, first at *Harper's* and then as editor in chief of *Vogue*. She helped millions of women understand that beauty and money aren't as important as intelligence and personal style. Vreeland put free choice back in style, toppling the "rules" invented by fashion designers. In the 1970s, in the last phase of her life, she became the first director of the Costume Institute at the Metropolitan Museum of Art, attracting thousands of new visitors to the museum.

Mini-Moontime Meditation: The Girl in the Mirror

Find a comfortable place where you can sit in front of a mirror by yourself. Using a brush, comb, hair pick, or your hands, comb through your hair. Some mystics believed that a woman's hair is her transmitter to the world — and to her spirit. As you comb through your hair, notice how beautiful it is. If you have any thoughts about it that you don't like, put them aside for now and just focus on appreciating your hair: the way it keeps your head warm on cold days, the way it blows in the wind, or how nice it is to braid and decorate with ribbons, bows, and barrettes. Feel how good it is to gently comb it.

Take a minute to look at the reflection of your eyes. Notice the small specks of light that bounce off your irises. Notice all their colors. See your lashes. Look at and touch your face — your eyes, nose, mouth, and skin. Think about how your nose lets you enjoy a fragrant day in spring. How your skin tingles on a cold morning or glows in the sunshine. Notice how your mouth lets you communicate when you need to, lets you say beautiful, kind things and express yourself. It lets you sing and share ideas. Eat nutritious food. Say surprising and shocking things. Your words can change the world!

Take a few minutes to really enjoy your reflection. Look at yourself and say, "I am beautiful" three times. Say it again until you can feel it without any doubts all the way into your belly.

You can take it up a notch: turn up some music and dance and sing in front of the mirror. Be a rock star or hip-hop dancer. Have a blast. Make up your own song about why you are the best thing to ever happen to this world. You are beautiful — through and through.

Remember, you are more than your face. You are more than your body. You are a beautiful, precious, wonderful young woman inside and out, and you are very loved!

Moontime Journaling: Finding Your Own Beauty Moments

A Journal Entry by Kelli, age twelve

Who am I?

I am beautiful because I give so much of myself to the world.

I am powerful because my spirit is strong and unconquerable.

I am great because I am committed to living my dream.

I am strong enough to endure the challenges of life.

I am really good at listening with an open mind and heart.

I really love to sing, climb trees, be barefoot and naked, laugh, and play.

I think my eyes are round, deep, and starry. They show my true feelings and my soul. I like my eyes because my sight is precious and my vision is honest and open and beautiful.

I think my ears are curly, small, and a delicate pink like a pig's tail. They are very sensitive. I like my ears because they feel good and allow me to hear.

I think my mouth is expressive and my lips are big. I have a beautiful voice that sails on the wind. I like my mouth because it allows me to communicate, to sing, to kiss, to laugh, and to eat.

Now, take out your moontime journal and complete the following sentences:

My mind is . . .

I like my mind because . . .

My hair is . . .

I like my hair because . . .

My eyes are . . .

I like my eyes because...

My nose is...

I like my nose because...

My ears are...

I like my ears because...

My mouth is...

I like my mouth because...

My hands are...

I like my hands because...

My arms are...

I like my arms because...

My heart is...

I like my heart because...

My breasts are...

I like my breasts because...

My stomach is...

I like my stomach because...

My hips are...

I like my hips because...

My butt is...

I like my butt because...

My vagina is...

I like my vagina because...

My legs are . . .

> *I like my legs because . . .*

My feet are . . .

> *I like my feet because . . .*

My body is . . .

> *I like my body because . . .*

My moontime is . . .

> *I like my moontime because . . .*

Moontime Magic: Inner Spring Cleaning

Sometimes, when I am not feeling great about my outsides, it means that I have been looking at too many magazines filled with pictures of airbrushed models and comparing myself to them (argh!), or that I am not thinking many good thoughts about myself. That means I need to do some "inner spring cleaning."

Take out a sheet of paper or your moontime journal and title it "What I Can't Stand about Things Right Now." Then list every single thing that is bothering you, anything that upsets you, everything that is bugging you. For example, maybe you hate all the clothes in your closet, or you hate that your friend scored higher than you on a test at school (and she didn't even study!), or you are mad that a boy at school isn't paying attention to you, and on top of all that you can't stand the president! Whatever it is, write it down. It is a huge relief to get it all out and not carry it around with you.

After writing the list, you might feel that's all you want to do. Or you could look it over and see if there is any one thing on the list that you could do something about — any situation that you could improve, anything that you could do that might make you feel better about it. For example, if you hate the clothes in your closet, you could take them all out, invite friends over with the clothes they no longer want, and have a clothing swap. Or you could sell them at your local consignment shop and use the money to build a new wardrobe. Taking action works like magic to help you feel better about yourself and your life. You have the power to make a change!

Sometimes, making changes on the inside by doing a little inner spring cleaning makes us want to do the same on the outside. Maybe it's time for a new haircut or style. Enjoy trying out new images of yourself. Experiment and have fun.

You are beautiful, no matter what they say.
Words won't bring you down.
You are beautiful, in every single way.
Yes, words won't bring you down.
Don't you bring me down today.

— Christina Aguilera, "Beautiful"

chapter 8

DREAMS
The Power of
Moontime Dreaming

The future belongs to those who believe in their dreams.

— Eleanor Roosevelt

Dreams are magical and surprising. They are doors we can travel through to reach whole new worlds. There are so many different kinds of dreams: daydreams, night dreams, lucid dreams, visions, and premonitions, to name only a few. Some women find that their dreams are more vivid or that they can remember them more easily at certain times of their cycle. Some women dream more while they are ovulating; others dream more during PMS; and still others dream more while they are menstruating.

When you dream, there are no limits. Everything is possible. In your dreams, awake or asleep, you might be an eagle soaring above the trees or a mermaid swimming in the deep blue ocean. In your dreams, you are completely free.

Native Americans believed that when a woman is menstruating, the veil between this world and the next is very thin and that it is now easier for her to dream and make contact with other dimensions. They believed that a woman's dreams during her moontime could tell the future of the tribe, and so the tribe treated her dreams and moontime as sacred.

Moontime Mythology: The Wisdom of Isis

In ancient Egypt, Isis was revered as a powerful goddess, a protector of children. Her mythology tells of how the evil god Seth cut Isis's husband, Osiris, into pieces that he scattered all over the land. Isis found and gathered the pieces of Osiris, magically restoring him to life.

The story of Isis reminds us that even when we feel our lives are falling apart, within us is the magic we need to restore ourselves and rebuild our lives.

In ancient times, people who honored the Goddess Isis would go to one of her temples to sleep and dream. Sleep restores our bodies and minds, and dreams can restore our emotions. Inside Isis's temples were mirrors. The mirrors were a reminder of the importance of self-reflection. In her temple, her worshippers tended their inner lives and reflected on the messages of their dreams.

The wisdom of Isis teaches us to pay attention to our dreams. They offer us insight every night, and by reflecting on them, we can be restored.

Dreaming Defined

Dreaming occurs in many different ways. The following are some general descriptions of various types of dreams.

- Daydreams: Daydreaming is the experience of letting your thoughts drift off and your imagination wander while you are awake. This could happen while you're sitting through a boring class or lying on the grass watching the clouds drift by.

- Night dreams: Every night as you sleep, your body enters different stages of sleep and dreaming. REM, or rapid eye movement, is an important sleep stage and is the time when most of your dreams happen. REM sleep allows your mind to let go of or dump all the events of the day, so that you can wake up refreshed and ready to take in a new day.

- Nightmares: Nightmares are dreams that can be frightening. Some common nightmares include being chased by someone while you are able to run away only in slow motion, or trying to scream but not being able to make a sound. Nightmares can be your mind's way of working out fears you have in your life. For example, when my niece was three years old, she dreamed that she was being eaten by a whale. Her best friend at preschool had a very overpowering personality and was physically stronger than she was. As she learned, with the help of both of their moms, how to say no to her friend when she felt overwhelmed, this nightmare went away.

- Lucid dreaming: Lucid dreaming occurs when you are asleep and dreaming and realize that you are dreaming and that you can influence the dream. For example, I had a recurring dream of being chased by a man. Then a friend told me that the next time I had the dream, I should confront the man and say, "Stop it." I wasn't sure how I could do this while sleeping, but I did. The next time I had the dream, I felt as if I woke up inside it and said, "Oh, yeah, I am having this dream again. Now I can turn around and tell him to stop." As I ran, I turned around, looked at the man, and said, "Stop chasing me!" At that moment, I grew into a giant woman and the man looked really small, the size of an ant. It was a great feeling.

When I journaled about it later, I wrote that I thought the man represented all the little daily things that I worried I couldn't handle. But when I took a minute to deal with them directly, I realized that they are little concerns — nothing that I can't handle!

Learning that I have control in my dreams and my nightmares has helped me with many challenges in my waking life.

- Visioning: Visioning might be a clear thought or feeling about something that hasn't happened yet. Some call this experience a *premonition*. You also vision when you consciously imagine something that you would like to come true. This is often called *visualization*, and it can be a tool for defining your goals and reaching them or for facing your fears and overcoming them. For example, you might envision yourself feeling completely relaxed and confident while speaking in front of your class, or hitting a home run for your softball team, or even waltzing down the halls of your school on the first day of your period, feeling completely carefree about cramps or stains. *Visioning* simply means purposely imagining something you would like to see happen in reality.

Moontime Herstory: The Gifts of Dreams

My dreams have always been interesting to me. I love trying to figure out their meanings and work with their messages. Sometimes the messages or gifts from my dreams are really clear to me, and other times they are much harder to figure out, but they are always valuable in some way. In fact, this book is the result of a dream I had. One night I dreamed that a "Great Mother" or goddess figure said to me all the things that I wish I had heard when I had my first moon and went through adolescence.

It was a beautiful dream. When I woke up, I wrote down everything that she had said. That was the start of this book.

Later, when I realized that I wanted to take those sweet words and create an entire kit that included a book and other items, like a journal and stickers, I started to visualize what the package would include. I visualized moms giving it to their daughters as a gift to celebrate their first moon. I visualized how it might be for young women to hear about celebrations from all over the world and about how incredibly special, beautiful, and celebrated they are.

I wrote the original draft, added illustrations and some sample gifts, and sent the kit off to publishers. Every week for several months, I visualized my book being published and imagined how I would feel when it was complete.

Initially, the book didn't find a publisher. I was disappointed, but I still kept my sample copy on my dresser, put a wish in my Goddess Box (see an explanation of Goddess Boxes in chapter 12), and went on with my life and other creative projects. Three years later, when I was least expecting it, a publisher called. She said she had received the book years earlier and that she loved it. So you are now reading the result of that sweet dream I had years ago. Getting to know your dreams and what they mean can take you on wonderful and unexpected journeys.

Create a beautiful space for sweet dreams. Surround your bed with pictures and items that make you feel good. Then let your dreams take your imagination, ideas, and goals to new heights.

How to Remember Your Dreams

Sometimes it can be hard to remember your dreams. Here are a couple of things you can do to make remembering them easy.

1. Take a small glass of water to bed. Just before you lie down to sleep, drink half of the water while saying to yourself, "When I drink the other half, I will remember my dreams." Upon waking, drink the other half, and you will remember your dreams. You might need to try this a few times to "train" your mind, but eventually it will work.

2. Keep a dream journal, or use your moontime journal, to record special dreams you want to remember. Once you get into the habit of recording your dreams, you will find that it becomes easier and easier to recall them.

Moontime Moments: Understanding What Your Dreams Tell You

Dreams often reflect themes — ongoing events and feelings — in your life. There are many common "dream themes," things that lots of people dream about. For example, many people dream of huge tidal waves. This can mean that a big change is coming or that strong feelings are rising to the surface. During transition times, this dream, or dreams of earthquakes, are common.

Learning to understand your dreams is a fun way to learn more about yourself. This is great, because the more you get to know and understand all the parts of yourself, the more comfortable and happier you will be and the easier it will be for you to understand other people. Purchasing a dream dictionary or checking one out from the library is a good idea. You can also seek out online dream dictionaries. In them, you can look up other common dream themes, like sleeping through the alarm on the day of a test at school, being naked in front of the class, falling, or flying.

Mini-Moontime Meditation: Bringing Your Dreams to Life

This might sound too simple to be true, but it really works. First, find a comfortable place to sit or lie down and relax. Take a few deep breaths. With each inhalation, imagine breathing in love and happiness. With each exhalation, imagine any worries or stresses leaving your body. Continue this for several breaths.

Now, resting quietly, think about something you would like to bring to life. For example, is there anything you really dream about doing? Publishing a book or a newspaper article, saving something important in your community or the environment, recording a CD? Whatever it is, let yourself ask for help on how best to achieve your heart's desire. Rest here and listen quietly for a response. It might come in the form of your voice in your head giving you advice, or as an image of a person you realize you could call on for support, or as some other symbol. Or the answer could come to you in a dream while you are sleeping. Once you have asked for help, trust that the answers and support will come. Just listen and look for the response.

When you are ready, bring your attention back to the present moment, stretch your body, blink your eyes, smile, and know your dreams are on their way to coming true!

Moontime Mythology: A Lakota Story of the Dreamcatcher Legend

Lakota wisdom tells us that long ago, when the world was young, an old man sat on a high mountain and had a vision. In his vision, Iktomi, the great trickster and teacher of wisdom, appeared in the form of a spider. Iktomi spoke to him in a sacred language that only the old man could understand.

As he spoke, Iktomi the spider took the elder's willow hoop, which had feathers, horsehairs, beads, and offerings on it, and began to spin a web. He spoke to the elder about the cycles of life, about how we begin our lives as infants and move on to childhood and then adulthood. Finally, we reach old age, when we must be taken care of as we were as infants, completing the cycle.

Iktomi said, "In each time of life there are many forces that can help or interfere with the harmony of nature, and also with the Great Spirit and all his wonderful teachings." Iktomi gave the web to the Lakota elder and said, "See, the web is a perfect circle, but there is a hole in the center of the circle. If you believe in the Great Spirit, the web will catch your good dreams and ideas and the bad ones will go through the hole. Use the web to help yourself and your people to reach your goals and to make good use of your people's ideas, dreams, and visions."

The elder passed his vision on to his people. Even today, many people use the dreamcatcher as the web of their lives. It hangs above the bed or elsewhere in the home to sift dreams and visions. The good parts of our dreams are captured in the web of life, but any bad dreams escape through the center hole.

Making a Dreamcatcher

Make your own special dreamcatcher to hang above your bed.
SUPPLIES YOU WILL NEED:

A 26-inch thin, round, basket-weaving reed
(available at a crafts store)
A 4-foot piece of string or twine
A 3-foot piece of yarn
Some beads, feathers, and/or crystals
Scissors

DIRECTIONS:

Step 1: Take a length of reed equivalent to approximately 26 inches, form into a circle, and secure by overlapping and bending the two loose ends around the edge of the circle. The circle width should be 5 to 5 $1/2$ inches. To strengthen the circle and prevent it from coming undone, you may tightly wrap the entire circle with a length of colorful yarn.

Step 2: To begin making the dreamcatcher "web," tie one end of the twine or string to the circle you formed in step one. Tie 9 "hitch knots" around the ring, spacing them approximately 2 inches apart. Keep the string snug when going from one knot to the next, being careful not to distort the shape of the circle.

Step 3: To begin the next row of the web, begin tying hitch knots in the middle of the string already attached. Continue tying hitches in the same way until the opening in the center is the desired size. To end the web, tie a double knot in the twine and cut off any excess.

Step 4: To decorate the dreamcatcher, you will need about 3 feet of string for attaching beads and/or feathers. Cut string into 4 equal pieces and thread the beads or tie the feathers to the ends. Tie these decorated strings to the bottom, sides, and center of the dreamcatcher. Be sure to attach a hanging loop to the top.

Sweet dreams!

Dreams bring you on many wonderful journeys. In dreams, you are completely free. You can fly, jump over tall buildings, and travel to other worlds. Many women notice that their dreams are more powerful and vivid at different times during their menstrual cycle. Sometimes dreams carry special messages and gifts for you. As you learn to pay attention and listen to your dreams, many magical things can unfold.

chapter 9

VISIONING & VISUALIZING
Bringing Your Dreams to Life

Your dreams and visions are your gifts to the world. By living them, you bring happiness and healing to others and give them permission to live their own dreams. By living your dreams and visions, large and small, you make the world a better place.

Ellen Ochoa, the first Hispanic female astronaut, reflects in an interview, "I can only imagine the amazement and pride my grandparents would feel, having been born in Mexico in the 1870s, on knowing that their granddaughter grew up to travel in space. Their move to the United States to raise their family, along with my mother's passion for learning, provided me with the opportunity to envision myself in outer space and motivation to get an education and set high goals. I encourage all Latinas and women to seek out interesting, challenging careers." Embrace your dreams, for your flights of fancy might turn into flights of much greater dimension.

What Is Visioning?

Visioning is the act of imagining and focusing on something your heart desires; it is a way to help bring that thing to life. Visioning or visualizing can help in every area of your life. Visioning clears the way for dreams to come true. Visioning helps you easily remove any barriers to achieving your goal, such as fears or other kinds of resistance. Visioning can be helpful for school, sports, relationships, and health, as well as for other things, such as becoming a rock star or working for world peace.

Visioning requires only that you set aside time each day (or week or even month) to think about exactly what you want. As you imagine what you want, fill in all the details: what it looks like, how it makes you feel. Leave the question of how it will actually happen for your spirit to figure out. While visioning, all you have to do is to imagine your dream as you really want it to be. Start carrying it around in your heart and thinking about it daily, believing it is possible. Every time you think of it, reassure yourself that this dream is coming to you. And absolutely believe that if it doesn't come, that is because something much better is on its way to you.

Our job as visionaries (people who vision) is to do our best to live healthy lives by caring for our minds and bodies and by enjoying ourselves completely and treating ourselves like the amazingly beautiful and magnificent queens that we are. We must each have the courage to dream big dreams, to vision them regularly, and to take steps to bring our dreams to life. The most important thing is that visioning is fun and pleasurable and brings you happiness. Then you know you are on the right track.

Women are creators. Each new thought we think, each new dream we dream, can be brought to life if we follow our natural cycle. The moontime cycle is like our bodies' own waterfall, washing away and cleansing that which we no longer need, connecting us to the Earth, making room for our visions, and bringing them to life. Fill your mind with beautiful music, art, and poetry. Create a fertile ground for your dreams to grow in!

Examples of Visioning and How to Do It

Have you ever heard the expression "Worrying is like praying for something you don't want to happen"? I love that saying. Our thoughts have a lot of influence on the rest of our lives. If we think good thoughts, especially about ourselves, chances are that we will have happy lives. If we think negative thoughts or worry much of the time, chances are that we will limit our happiness.

I like to visualize what I want instead of worrying about what I don't want. I do this for myself, for my friends and family, and for the world. Visualizing during your moontime can be especially nurturing, creative, and fun. Moontime is a natural time for reflection and quiet, and visioning is a very relaxing and sweet experience. Visioning during our moontime can do the groundwork for the rest of the month, so that when we are ready to take up our busy lives again, everything will unfold with grace.

VISIONING AND PARENTS

Visioning about issues you have with your parents is a fun exercise. For example, if you and your parents have been stuck in an argument that you don't know how to resolve, try visioning. When you have some time alone, close your eyes and relax. Let all your worries and frustration about this situation go. See yourself letting them go. Put them in a big red helium balloon and watch it float high into the sky, up and away. Good!

Now imagine yourself sitting with your parents in whatever place you usually talk together. Imagine that each of you is filled with love and support. Let yourself sit in these warm feelings. Imagine you can see the flow of love between you and your parents. Know that each of you wants to reach the best possible solution. In your meditation, tell your parents what you want them to hear. Share all your feelings with them. Then tell them that you trust that their decision will come from love only, because you know that you are loved no matter what. Now listen to see if they respond to you in your meditation. They might or might not.

When you bring your attention back to the present moment, try to also bring back all the good feelings of love and support. The next time you talk to your parents about the issue, notice if anything changes. You might be pleasantly surprised! Generally, when people try this, they may not *always* get the exact outcome they wanted, but they always have a much happier one.

VISIONING AND FRIENDS

If you are having trouble with a friend — for example, maybe you don't get along as well as you used to, or maybe she did something to hurt your feelings — try visioning.

As in the above example of visioning with your parents, first imagine that you and your friend are surrounded by love and support. Relax into that feeling. In your visualization, see yourselves speaking freely and with care to your friend. Let her know what is on your mind and in your heart. As you speak to her directly, remember and trust that this can work out. Now listen for her response. Notice what you feel in your body. Do you feel relieved, more relaxed, and happy?

Or maybe your friend is having a rough time and has shared with you that she is struggling with her parents or another friend. After you have supported her by listening, you can visualize good things for her. Instead of worrying, you can visualize her surrounded with love, support, and good feelings. You can see her laughing and having a very happy day. You can do this each morning for a week as a gift to her. Visualizing good things for the people we love feels really great.

VISIONING FOR HEALTH

Did you know that some hospitals now use medical intuitives to help patients heal and recover from surgery? *Medical intuitive* is another term for a healer — someone who might use "alternative" techniques for healing, such as visioning, massage, and other types of treatments. Medical intuitives are sometimes invited into the surgery room. During surgery, their job is to focus on or imagine the patient as completely healthy and whole and the surgery as going perfectly. Whether the technique is proven or not, patients treated by intuitives often feel so much better compared to those who aren't that doctors are starting to see the real value of visioning, both for yourself and for others.

Use visioning to imagine a perfectly healthy body or to heal from a wound or injury. Imagine the injury completely healed and well. Imagine any cramping from your moontime going away, and see all the muscles in your body relaxed and healthy. Visualize clear and radiant skin.

VISIONING FOR SCHOOL AND SPORTS

Visioning can help you improve your performance in many areas of your busy life. For example, you can use it to help you write a challenging paper or report. Imagine easily finding all the information you need to write the paper. See yourself having fun, enjoying the writing process, and turning the paper in on time. Imagine the completed paper and how you feel when you're finished. See the smile on your face.

Or you can vision for other purposes, such as preparing for a speech or performance. Use the same process. In your meditation, see yourself on the day of your presentation. See yourself surrounded by love and support. See how happy you look, feel how confident you are, and feel that confidence in your body. See how natural your performance is and that you easily remember everything. Imagine completing the performance and your relaxed and satisfied feeling. See people smiling around you.

You can definitely use visioning to alleviate any worries you have about getting your period at school. Visualize yourself playing sports, walking happily down the school hall, or at the school dance feeling great and totally confident in your tampon or pad's ability to prevent leaking.

Visioning is also perfect for sports. Some professional teams vision together while preparing for a big game. If you have a competition coming up, you can use visioning to see yourself easily making it over the hurdles in the track meet or to see your soccer team "in the zone," effortlessly working together to bring yourselves a victory.

Moontime Journaling: The Desire List

It's time to tell yourself what you want — *everything* that you want! Take out your moontime journal. Across the top of a blank page, write "My Desire List" and today's date. Next, list every single thing you want in your life. First write what you want, then affirm having it (see the examples on the next page). Hang a copy on your mirror or another place where you can easily refer to it. Look at it often. Each time a desire comes to you, check it off your list and write a new one. This is very satisfying and helps you to believe that following your heart's desire makes your dreams come true.

Examples of desires and accompanying affirmations:
I want a new puppy.
   I have a new puppy, and she is soooo cute.
I want some new earrings.
   I have beautiful new earrings that I love.
I want more time to hang out with my friends.
   We have so much great time together.
I want to take singing lessons.
   I love my new singing lessons.
I want to travel to faraway lands.
   I love traveling in India, Australia, and Brazil.
I want to feel happy in my body.
   I love the way my body looks and feels.
I want to accept myself just the way I am.
   I am pretty cool.
I want to get along better with my brother.
   My brother and I are good friends.
I want healing for my aunt who is sick.
   My aunt is healing.
I want the war to end.
   The war is over, peace and healing have begun.
I want to be included with my friends and to include others.
   I include others in all I do, and my friends include me.

GIRLS SHARE THEIR DESIRE LISTS

I visualize world leaders admitting when they are wrong and picking up pieces of the shrapnel in the Middle East.

I visualize sunshine and shelter so the homeless people I see won't have to sleep under benches to protect themselves from the cold rain.

I visualize my parents making up.

I visualize more happiness and less pain in the world.

I visualize myself in the future — a strong, brilliant woman.

Write down your visions or goals for next week, next month, next summer. Write down three things you can do that will help you reach each goal. Always ask for everything you want — you just might get it. Even if you are scared to ask for what you want or think that it might be too much, just by asking, you let other people help you figure out ways to get it!

Moontime Magic: Make a Special Place for Your Dreams to Come True

For centuries, the ancient Chinese art of *feng shui* has been used to promote harmony and balance in every area of life: wealth, relationships, family, romance, health, creativity, and travel. During your moontime, and when you're thinking about your visions, you might like to create a special place where you can just rest and recharge. Feng shui can help you do this.

Your bedroom is probably the perfect place. Decorating and setting up your bedroom to attract all the good stuff you want into your life can help your dreams come true. It's easy to "map" your bedroom according to feng shui principles. Here's how:

1. First, take time to clear out any clutter in your room. Go through your closets and give away anything you no longer want. Clean out your desk and your backpack, too.

2. Next, draw a roughly square outline of your bedroom on a piece of paper. The wall that has the main doorway to your room should be on the bottom of the square.

3. Divide the square into nine equal squares, three rows of three squares each.

4. Label the squares. The lowest row of squares represents the areas closest to your door. The left corner of the room (and of the square) is the area of knowledge. The center square relates to career, and the right-hand square is helpful people and travel.

5. Now label the central row of squares, which describes the middle of your bedroom. The left square relates to family and health. The central square is the *tao* (meaning place of balance and center), and the right-hand square is creativity and children.

6. Last, label the top row of squares. The left square relates to wealth, the central square to fame and reputation, and the right square to relationships and romance. Your layout should look something like this:

Wealth	Fame and Reputation	Relationships and Romance
Family and Health	*Tao*	Creativity and Children
Knowledge	Career	Helpful People and Travel

7. Here are objects that will work best in each area of your
    room, helping you to attract more of what you need:

- **Knowledge:** Bookcase, books, tools for self-development
  such as foreign language lessons on CDs, or how-to
  books on your favorite subjects. I keep books by authors
  that inspire me most.

- **Career:** Mirrors or water-related items; images that support your career goals. Hang pictures on your wall of
  women in the career field that you aspire to; if you want
  to be a doctor, hang a picture of a woman doctor.

- **Helpful people and travel:** Pictures of people who help you
  in life and of the places you want to explore.

- **Family and health:** Family snapshots, photo collages, and
  plants.

- **Creativity and children:** Art supplies, artwork, and/or your
  computer. I keep a box of crayons and pictures of my son
  and his cousins playing at a baseball game.

- **Wealth:** Money, jewelry, fish, or fountains; anything red,
  purple, or gold. This is a fun area to decorate. I have a
  ceramic bowl filled with foil-covered chocolate coins.

- **Fame and reputation:** This area represents how others per-
  ceive you in the world. Candles, awards, or plants; anything red, orange, or purple are all good suggestions. I
  have a framed list of qualities that I aspire to, such as
  "strong, fair, honest, creative," in this area of my room.

- **Relationships and romance:** Round or oval mirrors, anything
  pink, pictures of loved ones, paired objects (like two
  candlesticks or two crystals). I keep a pink orchid in this

corner, a picture of me with my boyfriend, and two match-
ing candlesticks.

Make your room as beautiful as you want, so that every time you
walk into it, you feel like a very special princess coming into your private palace, the place where your dreams are born.

Mini-Moontime Meditation: Think Good Thoughts

Find a comfortable place to sit or lie down, preferably on the earth.
Take a few deep breaths. Let your body relax with each exhalation.
Picture a beautiful crystal-blue waterfall at the top of your head.
Imagine the lovely water pouring into your head, washing through your
entire body, and pouring out into a stream that runs into the ground.
Let it wash away any thoughts that you no longer need, any problems
that are stressing you out, and anything that is bringing you down.
Now fill your mind's eye with a clear vision of what you want for
yourself. For example, imagine the kind of day you would like to have,
the kind of presentation you want to make at school, the part you'd like
in the school play, or the after-school job that you've been hoping for.
Make your vision as clear as possible, seeing all parts of the picture.
Now check in with your body. Imagine how your body will feel
when this vision becomes reality.

Visioning with Friends

Sometimes, I like to take turns visioning with a friend, especially
when I have a big-time vision to consider. We each share our vision

and then take turns visioning each other's dream together. This usually takes about five minutes per vision. When we finish, we talk about what we saw for each other and for ourselves in our vision. It is so much fun, and it's especially exciting when we both experience or see the same thing.

Visioning to Bring Your Dreams to Life

After I have visioned, I usually experience a lot of synchronicity. Synchronicity is the experience of being in the right place at the right time, or thinking about something you desire and suddenly everywhere you go and anyone you talk to mentions something related to your desire. For example, when I was visioning about this book, I met several women over the course of several weeks who did some kind of work with teenage girls, and some worked on the topic of menstruation. It's funny, the way life works. Visioning is a way to invite into your life all the people and situations that will help bring your dreams into reality.

Moontime Moments: The Vision Map

Vision mapping is another way to envision your dreams. It's especially fun to do with friends.

Gather several magazines. Then find a large piece of posterboard. Next, lie back and let your mind wander to your biggest dreams. Think of everything you want and dream of, and also think about the little everyday things you love.

When you are finished visualizing, sit up, open the magazines, and, for the next twenty minutes, cut out any pictures or images that remind you of the things you love, what is important to you, and, most of all, your biggest, wildest dreams. Glue the pictures on the posterboard in any way you choose. Share your vision map with a friend. Hang it on your wall, where it is easily in view each day, and watch as your dreams come true.

chapter 10

FRIENDSHIPS & CONNECTIONS
How They Change as You Grow

A First Moon Celebration Story

L isa was born in Iraq and lived there until she moved to the United States at sixteen. When Lisa was ten, she had her first moon. In her family, this was cause for great celebration — it marked Lisa's entrance into womanhood. Her mother let all her women relatives know that Lisa's first moon had arrived. Her grandmother adorned her in gold bracelets and necklaces. Faraway relatives sent gifts of gold. They celebrated Lisa's rite of passage throughout that entire year. Her grandmother told her that when she was menstruating, she should indulge herself with good things and treat herself extra-special.

When Lisa was sixteen and moved to America, she noticed that women didn't celebrate their periods in the same way and that they did not think as highly of their periods as she and her family in Iraq did.

Lisa, now in her early forties, never experienced PMS or cramps. It is thought that girls and women who treat themselves with care and celebrate their periods have much less PMS and cramping. Now Lisa's own daughter is eight. When she has her first moon, Lisa plans to make it special for her daughter, just as it was for her. She hopes that every month, she and her daughter will have a "mother-daughter" day to celebrate their womanhood and their connection and to do something relaxing and perfectly indulgent, just for the two of them — maybe go to a spa or get their nails done, maybe take a walk by the ocean. She hopes her daughter will like that, too.

Moontime Mythology: The Moon Lodge

In ancient times in many cultures, women went to a moon lodge or "menstrual hut" together during menstruation. This was a monthly time for women to be together, tell stories, and care for themselves. In the hut or lodge were young women who had just begun their menses, women of childbearing age, and women close to the end of the menstruating years, a time called *menopause*. They were all together for a few days each month.

In the moon lodge, women told stories about how to best care for their bodies, about coming of age, about their relationships, about childbirth, and about all the many experiences they had as women. Young girls were able to get an up-close view of what to expect. They were able to see changes occurring in the women's lives around them and to learn how to take care of themselves. By learning to trust their bodies' cycles and to allow feelings to emerge within themselves, young girls became women, some of them healers and visionaries for their tribes and villages.

Relationship Changes

Many girls experience changes in their relationships with others around the time of their first moon. You might notice that this time brings you closer to the women in your life. Having your first moon is something you can share with other girls and women — such as your friends, older sisters, mom, aunts, and grandmothers. But it is also a time when you might want more privacy or space from your mom or older sisters, and from your brothers or dad.

Sometimes girls sense that their parent or parents now treat them a little differently — like more of a grown-up. Parents can have mixed feelings about watching their daughters grow up. Mostly, parents feel full of love and happiness for their daughters, but they can also feel some sadness at seeing their little girls change into young women, just as they felt both joy and sadness when they watched them grow from babies into toddlers and from toddlers into little girls. Sometimes parents, especially fathers, want to be respectful of this amazing change in your life, and so they give you more space. This might be great, or it might be difficult.

Dads often try hard to act casual with their daughters about all these changes, but because a girl's changes are different from a boy's, they might not always say or do the best thing. Sometimes they need a little educating. If you think this is the case with your dad, you can talk to him about it, give him a book like this one, or ask him to talk to your mom or aunt about it.

You also might notice that you have new feelings for or attractions to your classmates. Maybe you have a crush on a kid in your class; whenever they're around, you feel happy or shy or both. This change, too, is normal, expected, and part of growing up. The best approach you can take is to just relax and try to enjoy these new feelings as much as possible. It's also good to pay attention to and respect all the feelings you have and to let the people around you know about them.

Just Girls' Time

"Girl time" is important and a lot of fun. It's a time to hang out and share first-moon stories and tales about other life experiences with your mom, other moms, aunts, sisters, and friends, and it is part of what makes being a girl so interesting and unique.

Being able to share your experiences, accomplishments, fears, and worries with other girls and women, and hearing stories about their experiences with moontime and coming of age, is a great way to learn the secrets of self-care. It's also super-fun to hear about all the silly stuff girls experience, to laugh and cry about it, to feel understood and offer understanding, and to feel connected. First-moon and coming-of-age stories are common to us all.

Girl time can also include walks with your mom or friends, having a slumber party or a girls' day at the beach, or just talking with your women relatives in the kitchen. Typically, girls and women like to gather around something beautiful or creative — for example, we like making a delicious meal together, working in the garden, or taking a hike high on a mountain to see a breathtaking view. You can also meet with other young women specifically to talk about the change you are all going through, to get support, to make friends, and to help one another's dreams come true.

GIRLS' CIRCLES

Several years ago, my sister Beth realized that she wanted to create a special space for her eleven-year-old daughter, Theresa, so that she could share her experiences in growing up. She wanted it to be a place that Theresa could count as all her own, where she could share with and hear from other girls and women. She also thought it was important that the space include something creative to do and that it be a sacred space, free of gossip and criticism, where girls could speak their minds and hearts, confident that what they shared would not be repeated outside and that they would be supported.

She erected a tent in her backyard and invited five of Theresa's girlfriends to come over for a "girls' circle" once a week for twelve weeks. Each week, the girls focused on a different theme or topic. These included body changes and body image, relationships, goals and dreams, peer pressure, ways to deal with conflicts and commu-nication, and values such as truth telling and fitting in. They also made art projects together, such as collages and life-size pictures of themselves.

Beth, Theresa, and Theresa's five friends loved the group and wanted it to continue, and so it did for the next two years. Each week they shared and listened to one another as they laughed, cried, and safely expressed all the newness in their lives. They supported one another with smiles and strength and beauty. Sometimes they role-played, which means to act out roles in fictional situations, to learn communication skills or ways to handle new situations. For example, role-playing can teach you how to say no to something a friend wants to do but you don't feel good about, or how to ask for something you want but are too afraid to request.

At about the same time, Beth met a woman who lived nearby. She had been doing the same thing with her daughter and daugh-ter's friends. After they met and told each other their experiences, they wanted to share their idea with other girls and moms all over the world, so they created the Girls' Circle Association. Now Girls' Circle trains moms, "other moms," teachers, and counselors all over North America to facilitate Girls' Circles. If you are interested in learning about creating a girls' circle for yourself or joining one nearby, go to www.girlscircle.com to learn more.

MOONTIME MOMENTS

"My Moontime Experience," by Fran, age fifteen

The years just before and after I got my period were the worst for me. After that, it was easier, and adolescence got slower, smoothing out each thing, and it still does. I think my best friend, Jennifer, was the biggest help in my life through the hard times. She was my diary and I was hers. No matter if it's your mom, a sister, or a friend, I think every girl needs another female to talk to and relate to during the time of her first period and all through that growing time. It is also important for self-esteem to not be alone in struggles.

One thing that made being ten years old hard was that I had already started puberty. At ten I needed a bra, and in my diary I would write about how I knew I needed one but really, really didn't want one. I also didn't want to talk to my mom about it at all. I would become very embarrassed when anything from deodorant to shaving legs to boys to bras came up, and I dreaded those moments.

I was eleven years old, almost twelve, when I got my first period. I was staying at my family's cabin with my aunt and uncle, my sister, and my cousins. On that particular afternoon, the only ones home were my sister Theresa (who is two years older than me) and my younger cousin Mary. I went to the bathroom and there it was. I was pretty unemotional about it. Probably a little scared and excited and annoyed, but mostly I saw it like it was: my first period, which would be a bit of a hassle from then on.

My sister and cousin were excited and eager to find me some pads and supplies. I remember my cousin exclaimed, "I am so glad I was here for this to happen so it can prepare me." Later, my aunt was excited, too, and she took me aside and told me I could ask for anything. She said that she was proud of me, that it was an exciting time in becoming a woman, and that my mom was coming up to the cabin the next day, so she'd leave the rest to her. I think her words were very sweet and supportive, though I was thinking more about how I hoped no one in the house was listening, and I kept my mouth shut and just nodded and said thank you. It was an embarrassing experience for me.

Nothing embarrassing happened. I just kept worrying about others knowing. Both my mom and I were pretty straightforward about it...you know... "Congrats, here are the pads and tampons, and good luck." I never really thought of what had happened as an honor to my body or to growing up. My mom wanted to celebrate with a dinner or a weekend with her or a girls' night or something, but I thought everything sounded cheesy and unnecessary.

I was frustrated that I could not swim, and this upset me and made my period an annoyance for the first year or even two. I was frightened of tampons for those first periods. I thought the idea of a tampon was incredibly uncomfortable and awkward. I think I was so worried about using tampons that even my body knew, because when I joined the swim team, I planned on not swimming in weeks when I had my period, but the entire season I never got my period once. Once I figured out tampons (and believe me, it took more practice than it should have), I never thought twice about it again, and I always use them.

Being so young and getting my period was part of why I was so reluctant to talk to my mom about it. It seemed so strange to me ...everything about puberty did, and though she offered talks often, I never really talked to her at all about anything. My friends were always the ones I talked to about periods and feeling awkward and all that stuff. After all, they knew exactly what I meant. I do wish

I had been able to be more open with my mom about it all, and I think that there isn't much more she could have done to make me that way. It just happened as it did.

Moontime Journaling: The Journal for the Generations

Besides your moontime journal, you might also want to create another kind of journal, a "journal for the generations." A journal for the generations is a book of your personal stories about being a girl and your first-moon experiences that you can pass along to other women relatives — your younger sister, cousins, nieces, or your own daughter someday. They can read your first-moon reflections, record their own, and pass it along in turn.

You can include anything in the journal that you think would be helpful or interesting for other girls to read. You could write about what it is like to be a girl at this point in history, about your dreams or your experiences during your moontime meditations, and about what your first moon experience was like.

For centuries, women passed on their wisdom about self-care, menstruation, sexuality, childbirth, healing, and well-being through storytelling. So, you might want to interview your grandmothers, mom, sisters, and aunts about their first moons and include their stories in your journal for the generations as well. Hearing the women in your family tell their stories will let you create your own family "herstory," and you can pass on their wisdom for generations to come by hearing and writing down those stories. Even if you find that your mother or grandmothers did not know about or pay much attention to the wisdom of the moontime cycle, you might still find valuable and interesting treasures.

When you interview your mom or your grandmothers, or both, about their first moon, ask how they cared for themselves, what they did/do during their moontimes, and what they might do differently if they could do it all again.

Mini-Moontime Meditation: Generations of Amazing Women

Find a comfortable spot to relax. Close your eyes and take a few breaths. Imagine yourself sitting in the middle of a circle of women. They are all holding hands around you, looking at you with love and admiration. You are happy to be with them in the center of this circle.

As you look closer at these women, you realize that they are the women of your family — your mother and sisters, your aunts, cousins, and grandmothers. They are also your great-great-grandmothers and their grandmothers. You realize that you are surrounded by generation upon generation of women, all connected to you through your family history. Each woman has her own story, her own dreams, her own sorrows, and her own magic. Now they are sending to you all the lessons they have learned, all their courage, their mistakes and successes, their wisdom and innocence, to support you in living your own dream.

As you imagine the many women who have come before you, feel their strength and power, which live on in you. Now it is your turn to live the life you imagine. When you are finished, gently open your eyes and move out into the world, confident in the knowledge that many women came before you and that you carry their spirit in your blood and bones, in your mind and heart.

Moontime Magic: Creating Magic Together

Girls, working together, can create magic. That magic can be as simple as helping a friend to feel better by listening to her concerns, or as huge as banding together to save the Earth. Create your own magic by having some special "girl time" each week or month.

Make a promise to support one another in life and to help one another remember to take good care of yourselves so that you can all live happy and outrageously magical lives. Read the promise below together, if you like.

TAKE THE GIRL PROMISE

I promise to always treat myself like the amazingly wonderful, gorgeous, brilliant queen that I am. I promise to take time out just for me each month. I promise to go after my dreams. I promise to ask for help when I need it. I promise to love myself more than anything . . . and I promise to support other girls as they do the same.

chapter 11

CONNECTING TO NATURE

 now the cycle of the moon is reflected in your body, connecting you to the greater cycles of life, welcoming you into your fullness as a woman.

Just as we are connected to other girls and women by our shared cycle, we are connected to the Earth, moon, sun, and stars around us. The Earth is a living being with cycles and seasons of her own. When we remember that we are part of the natural universe around us, we remember that, likewise, the universe is part of us.

Every morning when I wake up and open my eyes to those first few moments between night and day, when the world is still and quiet, I can feel the Earth alive and ready to give birth to a new day. As the stars fade from view and night gives way, I feel excitement and anticipation at what will happen in the world today.

Sometimes nature surprises me with a breathtaking painting, a sky filled with pinks and purples and rays of golden light. Sometimes I am showered with rain watering my garden, and lightning dances across the sky. Sometimes nature kisses me sweetly with a soft breeze on my face or the warmth of the sun on my skin and the sweet scent of jasmine in the air.

The times when I am out in nature, on my runs or hikes on mountain trails or beside the ocean, are the times I am most at home with myself, the times I am happiest. Nature is where I go to restore myself and dream. The Earth is full of gifts each day. No matter how I feel or what is going on in my life, I can always count on feeling better after I have spent time in the garden or on my runs, seeing, breathing, and feeling the Earth.

Nature's Mirror: The Butterfly Girl

I was a caterpillar, happy to be myself. And suddenly I started to feel inner pullings, some feeling inside that took me away from my life and my world. All I could do was make a room for myself — this small cocoon. I built it around me, soft and warm, so I could dream, though I didn't know of what or why. I decided I couldn't fight it, though I tried, and so I rested, and I dreamed of many things.

When I woke up, I noticed myself changing on the inside. And for a while I just stayed in my cocoon. But all at once I knew I had to push off and away from my cocoon and open up into the world. And as I did, I noticed that I had changed on the outside, too. I had wings filled with beautiful colors and designs — all unique just to me. And I flew out into the world, happily dancing with the flowers, enjoying their beauty and the beauty of myself.

Like the change from caterpillar to butterfly, your growth from a girl into a woman is a transition filled with new and unfamiliar things. If you listen to your "inner pullings" and care for yourself, you will happily emerge from this time as your beautiful, unique self. Seeing the way nature reflects the many changes we experience in life can be helpful. The more comfortable we are with cycles and seasons, life and death and rebirth, times for turning inward and times for shining in the world, the happier we will be.

Moontime and the Phases of the Moon

Every month, the moon, like our own bodies, goes through phases. The lunar cycle repeats itself every 29.5 days; the average menstrual cycle lasts about 28 days. In ancient times, when there was no electric lighting, women who lived near one another menstruated together on the new or dark moon. Just as sunlight and moonlight affect plants and animals, our hormones were triggered by levels of moonlight. Women were aware that their natural cycles happened in synchrony with the moon's phases. Ancient cultures that celebrated and worshiped goddess figures believed that they were embodied in the Earth, the universe, and particularly the moon. Moon cycles were seen as reflecting the natural rhythm of a woman's body and life passages. Just as the moon is receptive to the sun's light and reflects that light to Earth, so the energy of the feminine was seen as receptive and reflective.

In Greece, the phases of the moon were given the names of goddesses: Diana for the waxing phase, Selene for the full phase, and Hecate for the waning period. These names mirrored the stages of women's lives: youth, maturity, and old age. The new moon symbolizes beginnings and birth, the waxing moon represents the period from childhood to menarche, and the waning moon mirrors the celebration of menopause and aging.

Science suggests that our body's cycles as well as dreams and emotional rhythms are connected to the moon, the tides and the planets. The moon and its tides interact with the energy fields of our bodies, and that has an effect on our physical, emotional, and dream lives.

Like the dark phase of the moon, women have times when they need to draw their attention into themselves, and, like the full moon, they have times to shine brightly in the world. Each woman has her own rhythm. The dark moon is the bleeding time, and the full moon is the time of ovulation. Though your own cycle might not exactly follow the phases of the moon, you might find yourself feeling more internal (like the dark moon) while you are bleeding and feeling more external when you are ovulating.

The menstrual cycle, because it connects to the lunar cycle, is a monthly reminder to see how you and all of us are intricately connected to the universe's greater cycles.

Moontime Moments: Tracking the Moon

By tracking the moon in relation to your cycles, you can learn to better understand the variations in your feelings and energy throughout the month.

On the first night of your period, note the size and location of the moon. You can track your period and the progress of the moon on the same dates until your period ends. This will help you compare your personal cycle to that of the moon.

Pay attention to your body and your emotions, and you might notice that you experience the same feelings at around the same time each month. As women, our bodies are aligned with the cycles of the natural world. Making that connection can be a powerful experience.

Moontime Magic: Your Secret Garden

Gardens are magical places full of new life and beauty. In the garden grow herbs that heal and nourish us, flowers that beautify our lives and give off amazing scents, and vegetables that feed us so that we grow healthy and strong. Creating your own secret garden where you can water and nurture your dreams is a beautiful way to connect with nature.

The fall, when leaves are falling from the trees and the Earth is preparing for her winter sleep, is a perfect time to plant some flowering bulbs. First, get your bulbs (such as tulips or irises), some rich soil, and a planter box or a little spot of earth. You can find a spot in your yard or, if you don't have access to a yard, fill a planter box with soil and keep it outside on your deck or at your front door. You might also want some gardening gloves and a small hand shovel (but I like to use my bare hands and get muddy). Ask your parents if they have any bulbs you can use, or go to a nursery and pick out your favorite types of bulbs and the other necessary items.

As you plant the bulbs in the rich soil (bury them about three inches down), think of any dream you might have, perhaps something you are working toward during this new school year. Maybe it is a dream of feeling comfortable in your own skin, or of being in the school play the following spring. Maybe you dream of being closer to your family or friends. Whatever it is, as you plant and care for your bulbs over the coming months — watering them when necessary — think of your dream.

Sometimes, when we are preparing for our dreams to come true, we don't think very much is happening. We don't seem to change much on the outside or see any results. Sometimes you might think you are doing everything you can, but nothing is happening. But like the bulb underground, there is a lot going on; it just needs time in the soil before it is ready to enter the world.

Our creative imagination works that way, too. Ideas need time to grow and take root, to become strong and secure, before they see the light of the sun. Always trust that even if you can't yet see the results, all your dreaming and hard work will soon come to fruition.

When you see the beauty of your garden next spring or summer, when all the flowers bloom, remember that you are looking at the beauty and magic of creation that live inside you. You are seeing and experiencing your own creation, loveliness, and grace.

Mini-Moontime Meditation: Flowering Girl, Flowering Woman

Find a comfortable place to sit on the ground, perhaps in your secret garden. Make yourself comfortable, either lying on the grass or sitting against a tree. Close your eyes. Take some deep breaths into your belly. Good. Just for now, let your day go.

Take in the scents and sounds of the Earth around you. Feel the air on your face. Remember that the oxygen you breathe is created by the Earth's plants and trees and by the sunlight. Take another breath and let everything else on your mind go.

Let yourself melt into the Earth. Feel the Earth below supporting and holding you.

Imagine a root growing from your womb down into the Earth. Like the roots of the strong redwood tree, let your roots grow deep into the soil. Good. Now imagine the warmth and energy of the Earth traveling up your roots and into your body. Notice how strong you feel when you are connected and rooted to the Earth.

Let the energy travel through your whole body, to the tips of your fingers and toes, up through your belly and throat, and out through the top of your head.

Imagine that your head is like the bud of your favorite flower. As the sun nourishes the flower, let it bloom, petal by petal, opening up to the blue sky above. Feel the light of the sun as it reaches your flowering head and flows into your body.

Now the energy of the Earth is flowing through your body, connecting you to the soil, grounding you and your visions. The energy of the sun is connecting you to the sky and your spirit; it is sharing your beauty and gifts with the world.

Moontime Journaling

Take out your moontime journal. Write about your mini-meditation, then complete the following sentences.

If I were a flower, I would be a..., because...

If I were a tree, I would be a..., because...

I see myself as most like the: ocean? sun? sky? Earth? wind? because...

My favorite thing to do in nature is...

I am grateful for the Earth because...

A JOURNAL ENTRY BY LIZZY, AT AGE SEVENTEEN

Before I get my period, right in the eye of my personal PMS storm, I have moments when all I want to do is write. The following passage comes from a journal entry I made during such a time, which I later used as part of an essay in college.

The Earth has her own cycles. She cries in the spring, only to see barren trees ripen and turn green; she succumbs to the heat of the summer, cracking and peeling bark off her limbs. Softly shivering in the autumn, she changes colors and slowly sheds layers; in the winter she sleeps naked, covered by city streets, city lights, city buildings, and a blanket of frost, only to wake up again and find insects sipping at her sweet nectar and gently pollinating her petals painted in every hue. The sun rises and falls; the waning crescent moon waxes and is full; the tide is high and then low.

Each of us leads a very different life. But despite these differences, we are all tied to the Earth and her cycles by the flow of energy of our own cycles. We are all born through a body that was brought into this world by another; girls become women and boys grow into men; and we need each other in order to continue in the circle of life.

One day, we will all leave these bodies and continue onward, only to once again become a part of something bigger than these seconds and these minutes, bigger than these days and years.

Life is a gift, a windy road of lessons and speed bumps, stop signs, dead ends, and turnarounds. We begin with the longest short passage we will ever experience in our lives, and we enter the world with a blinded gasp, wriggling and new. We spend our lives trying to figure everything out, not quite knowing what we are searching for but still searching because somebody once told us that there is always something better than this. We laugh and cry; we win and we lose; we love hard and fall even harder, only to pick ourselves up, dust ourselves off, and start all over again.

chapter 12

CONNECTING TO YOUR SPIRIT

A bird doesn't sing because it has an answer,
it sings because it has a song.

— Maya Angelou

Now that you have learned to care for yourself and are taking time for your inner self, you are ready to go out and *shine*. Like the moon, there are times when you can be hidden from the world and times when you can shine full and bright.

Your spirit is the shining part of you that is strong and unconquerable. Your spirit is whole, perfect, and complete. Your spirit connects you to your talents and dreams, to your visions and inspirations, to nature and your community. Your spirit *is* you.

Moontime Herstory: Mia Hamm

Everyone has a talent, and God gave me the athletic ability and competitiveness to go out there and push myself. It would be a disservice to myself if I couldn't be the best athlete and best person I could be.

— Mia Hamm

Mia Hamm, the thirty-two-year-old soccer superstar, is an example of an unconquerable and beautiful spirit. Playing soccer was all she ever wanted to do. At age six, on an all-boys' team, she was the best athlete she could be. She went on to become the youngest member of the U.S. women's national team at fifteen; she helped lead the team to a victory of the first Women's World Cup at nineteen; and, in 2000, she helped found the first-ever women's professional soccer league.

Today, she is considered a role model for both girls and boys. Hamm rarely gives interviews and when she does, she talks mostly about her teammates. Her modesty is perhaps partly due to the fact that she has faced challenges and tragedy. Born with a partial club-foot, Hamm had to wear a painful brace for a few years as a child. Far worse, her adopted brother Garrett, whom she loved very much, died in 1996 following a bone marrow transplant for a rare blood disorder. To channel her pain positively, she started the Mia Hamm Foundation, dedicated to supporting bone marrow disease research.

Seeing Spirit in Yourself and in Your Community

Connecting to our dreams and visions in our community often gives us an opportunity to see our spirit. Maybe one of your dreams is to heal the Earth or to help build a better school. By connecting with other people in your school or community to take action and make that dream a reality, you can witness the strength and magic of your spirit in the world.

KASSIE'S STORY

Kassie grew up in a family that did not know very much about caring for the environment. When she was in middle school, her science teacher taught her class about the importance of recycling and how it helps the Earth. Kassie taught her parents about it, and they set up recycling containers in their home.

Kassie and her parents felt good about the fact that, in their own small way, they could help the environment. Kassie continued to learn about caring for the environment and about easy choices people can make to create a healthier Earth. She learned about things that cause pollution and that one of the biggest causes of pollution in the United States is the generation of electricity from coal and fossil fuels. Kassie learned about *renewable energy* — energy made from sunshine, wind, water, and other nonpolluting natural resources. Using renewable energy to generate electricity made sense to Kassie. Kassie found herself more and more passionate about wanting to make a change for the environment.

When she went to college, she met a girl named Sara, who was also passionate about stopping pollution. Together they started a student movement to get their college to buy electricity made from renewable energy sources instead of polluting energy sources like coal and nuclear power plants. After two years of their hard work, their college became one of the first colleges in the nation to do this. Now many others are doing the same. Today Kassie has a career in renewable energy and trains college students all over the United States in how to get their schools to switch to renewable power.

Kassie followed her interests and her heart and teamed up with another woman, and together they made a major change in their school community to help the Earth. Kassie followed her spirit and is now working in a job she loves, changing the world one college at a time.

Mini-Moontime Meditation: You're a Superstar

Close your eyes. Bring your attention to your heart. Take a few deep breaths. When you are relaxed, imagine you are staring up at a starry sky. Let your eyes wander the sky until you notice a star that is drawing your attention to it. See how it grows brighter and brighter. Notice that you can feel its warmth filling up your body.

Imagine that you and the star are coming closer together — and that now you are filled with the star. It is living in your heart. It is bright and beautiful. Let its warmth fill your body. Let its golden light fill you up and shine out into the room around you. This is you. This is your power and strength and light. This is where all your dreams live. It is your own treasure.

You can play with your star's brightness and decide when you want it to shine brightly in the world for everyone to see and when you want to keep it close inside, just for yourself to smile about. Know that wherever you go, you carry around this beautiful light — you are a superstar.

Moontime Journaling: If I Could Change the World, I Would

Take out your moontime journal. Imagine and respond to the following scenarios:

1. The leaders of world have called upon you to be in charge for the year. What are the first five things you'll do? Why?

2. Imagine yourself at the ripe old age of ninety-three. You are a very wise old lady indeed. You have many important words of advice to share with your younger self. You have

lived an amazing, over-the-top life. Write a letter from your ninety-three-year-old self to yourself today, telling you the five most important things to do during your life.

Moontime Moments: Spirit in Action

There is an expression that goes, "Think globally, act locally." This means that maybe there is something you would like to change for the whole world, and that by taking action close to home, you can take the first steps toward making a larger change. Other people are working on similar things in their communities. One by one, communities around the world can make big changes for the whole world.

How do you get started? Here are some basic steps to follow:

1. Brainstorm. Write down one thing you would like to change in your world. Think about others who might be interested in this, too.

2. Get people together. Look for people who are interested in and passionate about the cause and who are willing to make a commitment of time and energy. Find an adult or organization to help you. You will need their resources to make your plan a success.

3. Make a plan. Set the goals for your project. Write them down clearly, and make sure that every person agrees on them. Decide when and where your group will meet. Make a schedule for the steps of the project. Decide if the project needs money and, if so, how much and how you will raise it. Let people know about the project, and if needed, get permission for everyone to participate.

4. *Put your ideas into action.*

5. *Evaluate what you did.* Together, write down and respond to the following questions:
   What did we like about our project?
   What would we do differently the next time?

6. *Share your success.* Send thank-you notes and letters of achievement to everyone involved in your work.

7. *Celebrate your success.* Have an end-of-the-project party. Make special awards for all the participants.

Moontime Magic: How to Use Your Goddess Box

This book came in a keepsake container that can be customized to be your very own Goddess Box. First, bless it with your own personal "goddessness" to make it all your own. Decorate it with the stickers included here, gel glitter pens, and more of your own favorite touches.

Your Goddess Box is the keeper of your dreams. Every time you think of something that you really want, make a wish or say a prayer to your angels, to nature, or to whomever or whatever you pray to, and write that wish down. For your most special dreams and wishes, dip into your best stationary, or find an extra-pretty bit of paper to write your wish on. Fold it up, seal it with a kiss, and place it in your Goddess Box. Check back by looking into your Goddess Box every few weeks or months to see how your dreams are progressing.

chapter 13

THE SECRET OF SUCCESS
Celebrating Yourself
Each and Every Day

What a Girl Knows and Can't Deny

Every girl has a secret. It's the best secret ever. It lives inside her. It is brilliantly bright and beautiful. It is pure happiness.

Every girl is born with a treasure inside, and she has a built-in map for finding it. If she takes care of herself by following her natural cycles and listening to herself and what she needs, she will easily find her hidden gold — and share it with the world.

She can imagine and create amazing things. Girls are gifted with the power to create their heart's desire: a beautiful life, and an amazing world. It is in girls' spirits, bodies, and dreams. It is the power of creation.

Moontime Herstory

One day I told my girlfriend that I just didn't think there was anything that unique about me. I didn't know what my gifts or my dreams were. She said that I had to start walking around like I had the best secret ever. She told me to smile a secret smile to myself and to other people, and that every time I did so, I should say to myself, "I have a really good secret." I didn't know what she meant. But I tried it, and it made me feel pretty good, so I kept it up.

Now I know what she meant. The secret she talked about is the gift that lives in me and in you. We all carry marvelous secret treasures: our spirit, imagination, dreams, and courage, mixed with the magic of creation.

Now that you have come this far, there's no doubt that you are a shining star. I hope you are celebrating yourself every day, and taking time each month for your own special recognition and retreat. Be good to yourself in all that you do. Dream big, reach high, and take heart in knowing that you are connected to the Earth, the moon, the sun, and the stars. You are connected to the legacy of generations of capable women who have done wondrous things in the world.

It all starts from a little self-care. Trust yourself and remember to ask for help when you need it. Surround yourself with visionary and kind women and men, with laughter and good friends, with beautiful art and music that make you want to move and groove, and while you're at it, be sure to wink at the moon.

If you know yourself and love yourself, you will always be cared for and celebrated each and every day.

A SIMPLE GLOSSARY OF TERMS

biodegradable: Ecologically friendly; will disintegrate naturally into the ground.

cervix: A part of a woman's internal genitalia; the entryway to the uterus.

endometrium: The tissue that lines the uterus.

estrogen: A hormone produced by mature eggs, or ova. Estrogen gives signals for breasts to begin to develop and pubic and underarm hair to grow, along with other, more subtle, changes like making the uterus grow.

external female genitalia, or vulva: Organs of the female reproductive system that you can easily see when you look between your legs; they are located outside the body. These include the labia majora, labia minora, clitoral hood, and clitoris.

feminine hygiene products, or menstrual protection products: Tampons, pads, and other products used to catch menstrual flow.

first moon: Menarche — the time of your first menstruation.

hormones: Chemicals made in the body that tell various organs how to develop and work. The body makes many hormones, and they play a role in almost all puberty changes: growth spurts, breast development, pubic hair growth, skin changes, and menstruation.

hymen: A thin tissue covering the opening to the vagina.

internal genitalia: The internal organs of the female reproductive system, located inside your body. These include the cervix, uterus, ovaries, and fallopian tubes.

labia majora: The outermost part of the vulva. Also called the outer lips.

labia minora: The innermost part of the vulva. Also called the inner lips.

medical intuitive: Another term for a healer. Someone who may use alternative techniques for healing, such as visualization and prayer.

menarche: The first onset of menstruation.

menopause: The phase of life when menstruation stops. When a woman reaches a certain age, usually her late forties to early fifties, her ovaries stop producing an egg each month. She no longer has a period or is able to become pregnant.

menses: The three to seven days a month when your body releases menstrual fluid.

menstrual flow: Another term for menstrual fluid.

menstrual fluid: The blood that exits the body during menstruation. menstruation and menstrual cycle: The complete monthly cycle.

moontime: The three to seven days a month when your body releases menstrual fluid.

os: The small opening in the cervix, leading to the uterus.

ova: Also called eggs, these are stored in the ovaries and contain genetic information. After release from the ovaries, if ova are met by sperm, fertilization occurs, resulting in pregnancy.

ovaries: Organs of the female reproductive system that contain the ova, or eggs.

ovulation: The monthly release of a mature egg from an ovary.

period: The three to seven days a month when your body releases menstrual fluid.

pregnancy: Once an egg has been fertilized by a sperm and the fertilized egg has attached itself to the uterine wall, pregnancy has begun. A full-term pregnancy (meaning the baby is fully developed by its end) lasts nine months and results in the birth of a baby.

progesterone: A hormone produced from the sac containing the egg, or ovum, that tells the uterus to thicken its lining and prepare for a possible pregnancy.

puberty: The name for developmental changes, both physical and emotional, that happen between the ages of eight and sixteen. Hormones (chemicals produced by our bodies) cause these changes.

urethra: The very small opening through which your urine passes.

uterus: The womb; the internal organ that holds a pregnancy.

vaginal opening: The beginning of the internal reproductive system. In many girls, the opening is partially covered by the hymen, a thin tissue.

visioning or visualizing: The act of imagining and focusing on a goal during meditation as a way to help bring that goal to life.

vulva: The external female genitalia.

BOOKS & OTHER RESOURCES

Barclay, Shinan, and Mary Dillon, with Elizabeth Manley (illus.). *Flowering Woman: Moontime for Kory (A Story of a Girl's Rites of Passage into Womanhood).* Sedona, AZ: Sunlight Productions, 1988. The extract in chapter 4 is drawn from pp. 18–19.

DeHaas, Cherie. *Natural Skin Care.* New York: Avery Penguin Putnam, 1987. The recipe for the Fresh Fruit Facial Cleanser in chapter 3 is adapted from p. 44.

Garfield, Patricia. *Dream Catcher: A Young Person's Journal for Exploring Dreams.* Toronto: Tundra Books, 2003. The story of Isis in chapter 8 is adapted from p. 34.

Jukes, Mavis. *It's A Girl Thing: How to Stay Healthy, Safe, and In Charge.* New York: Alfred A. Knopf, 1996.

Kaminski, Patricia, and Richard Katz. *The Flower Essence Repertory: A Comprehensive Guide to the Flower Essence Research by Dr. Edward Bach and the Flower Essence Society.* Nevada: Earth-Spirit Inc., 2000.

Katzen, Mollie. *The Enchanted Broccoli Forest.* Berkeley, CA: Ten Speed Press, 1982, 1995. The recipe for Super Sassy Soup in chapter 3 is adapted from the Inspiration Soup recipe on p. 27.

Lehrman, Karen, and IZAK (illus.). *Wise Women: Inspiring Words and Stories to Guide You to Be Your Best.* Des Moines, IA: Meredith Publishing, 2003. The information in the Frida Kahlo, Diana Vreeland, and Mia Hamm "Herstories" in chapters 3, 7, and 12 are adapted from pp. 33, 79, and 87.

Levitt, Susan. *Teen Feng Shui.* Rochester: Inner Traditions, 2003. The feng shui decorating suggestions in chapter 9 are adapted from www.susanlevitt.com.

Making a Dreamcatcher: http://www.teachersfirst.com/summer/dreamcatcher.htm. The dreamcatcher instructions in chapter 8 are adapted from this website.

Madaras, Lynda, with Area Mandas. *The What's Happening to My Body Book for Girls: A Growing Up Guide for Parents and Daughters.* New York: New Market Press, 1983, 1988, 2000.

Northrup, Christiane. *Women's Bodies, Women's Wisdom.* New York: Bantam, 1998. "The Goddess Menses" story in chapter 1 is adapted from pp. 147–148.

Rutter, Virginia Beane. *Celebrating Girls: Nurturing and Empowering Our Daughters.* Berkeley, CA: Conari Press, 1996. The Navajo celebration ritual in chapter 2 is adapted from pp. 110–111.

Worwood, Valerie Ann. *The Complete Book of Essential Oils and Aromatherapy.* Novato, CA: New World Library, 1991.

Information Resources

The following is a list of helpful body, mind, and spirit resources for girls.

Department of Health and Human Services: www.4Girls.gov. This site focuses on friends and family relationships, trust, sexuality, violence and abuse, peer pressure, and self-esteem. The site is a resource that responds to adolescent girls' health concerns. The purpose of the site is to motivate girls to choose healthy behaviors without the tediousness of "you should do this" messages.

Feminist Women's Health Center: http://www.fwhc.org/teens/index.htm

First Moon Ceremonial Kit: www.celebrategirls.com

GirlPower Project: www.girlpower.gov

Girls' Circle Association: www.girlscircle.com

Terra Grace: www.terragrace.com. This site provides health resources and healing products derived from flower essences and essential oils. Flower essences and essential oils address many different mental and emotional aspects of healing. Moontime Oils are made for girls and women to use during menstruation. Powerful Potions are made specifically for children who are especially receptive to their healing qualities. Helping children through everyday rough spots, Powerful Potions can address fears and stress and can boost concentration and self-esteem. Terra Grace offers a *First Moon* link that girls can use to share their own moontime stories, visions, and dreams with each other in an interactive virtual moon lodge.

Product Resources

Ecologique Natural Spa Essentials: www.ecologique.com. Sells
flower essences and essential oils.

Feminine Options: www.feminineoptions.com. Sells washable cloth
menstrual pads.

Glad Rags: www.gladrags.com. Sells soft organic cotton cloth
menstrual pads.

Jade and Pearl: www.jadeandpearl.com. Sells organic sea sponge
tampons.

Johnson & Johnson: www.cyclesofwellness.com. Sells Stayfree
pads, Carefree panty liners, and o.b. tampons.

LunaPads International: www.lunapads.com.

Manymoons: http://pacificcoast.net/~manymoons/moons.html.
Sells washable pads.

Moontime Oils: www.terragrace.com. Sells blends of flower
essences and essential oils specifically for moontime.

Natracare: www.Indra.com/natracare. Sells non-chlorine-bleached
disposable pads and tampons.

Organic Essentials: www.organicessentials.com. Sells organic tampons.

Pandora Pads: www.pandorapads.com. Sells organic cotton cloth
menstrual pads and tampons.

Procter & Gamble: www.tampax.com and www.always.com. Sells
Tampax tampons and Always pads.

ThermaCare: www.thermacare.com. Sells air-activated heat wraps.

ACKNOWLEDGMENTS

With special thanks first and foremost to the great mother goddess for inspiring me with a sweet dream. To my nieces, this one's for you. To my mom, sisters, aunts, grandmothers, and the generations of women that came before, thank you for passing on your faith, courage, love, wisdom, and humor. To my dad, brother, and nephews, thank you for teaching me persistence and living with a big heart. To Elizabeth Peterson, niece and goddaughter extraordinaire, thank you for your constant support and early editing. To Virginia Beane Rutter, thank you for your thoughtful feedback. To Vanessa Brown, my fabulous gift editor, and art director Mary Ann Casler, thank you for seeing this vision and bringing it to reality. To Laura Harger, thank you for your great work and insight. Thank you Kai for your sweetness, ideas, huge support, and overall amazingness. Thank you Kirk for your love. Thank you Leslie, Rochelle, Susan, Vickie, Lizzie, Nancy, Wende, and Amy. And special thanks to the women and girls in this book who gave their heartfelt stories and inspiration — and all the girls who continue to inspire us with their lives each and every day.

ABOUT THE AUTHOR

Maureen Theresa Smith is a writer, development director (for an environmental nonprofit), entrepreneur, and healing arts professional living in Marin County, California, with her eleven-year-old son, Kai. For her college thesis project, Maureen facilitated Adolescent Girls' Self-Esteem Circles and researched supporting girls' self-esteem through community action and connection to nature. Her company, Terra Grace Productions, creates blends of essential oils and flower essences and offers a unique line specifically for children and teens.

Maureen's life's work has been learning how to integrate spirituality into everyday practices and rituals that are inspirational and fun, in order to support girls and women in becoming whole strong women. She focuses on offering support and guidance to girls and women as they transition from one phase of their lives to the next. Her work incorporates a range of healing modalities, including flower essences, aromatherapy, financial planning, visioning, and life coaching.